Grammar for Literacy

CfE

Jane Cooper

students & teachers
FOR OVER 100 YEARS

HODDER
GIBSON
AN HACHETTE UK COMPANY

The Publishers would like to thank the following for permission to reproduce copyright material.

Photo credits

p.5 (left) © tilialucida – stock.adobe.com, (middle) © ERIC – stock.adobe.com, (right) © Nabil BIYAHMADINE/Fotolia.com; **p.11** © mRGB – stock.adobe.com; **p.16** © Riko Best – stock.adobe.com; **p.21** (left) © ChantalS – stock.adobe.com, (middle) © tracyhornbrook – stock.adobe.com, (right) © spflaum – stock.adobe.com; **p.22** © Annuitti/Shutterstock.com; **p.32** (top) © Stockcity – stock.adobe.com, (bottom) © piyathep – Fotolia.com; **p.35** © THANAGON – stock.adobe.com; **p.51** © B-DIZZY – stock.adobe.com; **p.80** © silvergull – Fotolia.com; **p.109** © zlikovec – stock.adobe.com; **p.122** © vickey – stock.adobe.com.

Acknowledgements

Every effort has been made to trace all copyright holders, but if any have been inadvertently overlooked, the Publishers will be pleased to make the necessary arrangements at the first opportunity.

Although every effort has been made to ensure that website addresses are correct at time of going to press, Hodder Gibson cannot be held responsible for the content of any website mentioned in this book. It is sometimes possible to find a relocated web page by typing in the address of the home page for a website in the URL window of your browser.

Hachette UK's policy is to use papers that are natural, renewable and recyclable products and made from wood grown in well-managed forests and other controlled sources. The logging and manufacturing processes are expected to conform to the environmental regulations of the country of origin.

Orders: please contact Hachette UK Distribution, Hely Hutchinson Centre, Milton Road, Didcot, Oxfordshire, OX11 7HH. Telephone: +44 (0)1235 827827. Email: education@hachette.co.uk Lines are open from 9 a.m. to 5 p.m., Monday to Friday. You can also order through our website: www.hoddereducation.co.uk. If you have queries or questions that aren't about an order, you can contact us at hoddergibson@hodder.co.uk

First published in 2021 by
Hodder Gibson, an imprint of Hodder Education
An Hachette UK Company
50 Frederick Street
Edinburgh EH2 1EX

Impression number	5	4	3		
Year			2025	2024	2023

Cover photo © nick76 - stock.adobe.com
Illustrations by Judy Brown/D'Avila Illustration Agency and Aptara, Inc.
Typeset in India by Integra Software Services Pvt. Ltd., Pondicherry, India.
Printed in the UK by CPI Group Ltd

A catalogue record for this title is available from the British Library.

ISBN: 978 1 3983 1188 6

SCOTLAND EXCEL

We are an approved supplier on the Scotland Excel framework.

Find us on your school's procurement system as *Hachette UK Distribution Ltd or Hodder & Stoughton Limited t/a Hodder Education.*

Contents

Getting the most from this book

There are several ways that you might use this book. Whichever approach you take, you will be able to navigate with confidence by following the icons and headings explained below.

You might use it in school with a class. A teacher might plan **regular lessons** on grammar and language throughout a term or a year. If you are using the book this way as part of a class or group, there are certain tasks that are designed especially for you. You will recognise them when you see this icon and box:

 Group task

You might use the book in school but use just **certain parts at certain times**. Your teacher might feel that the whole class would benefit from learning about, or revising, one aspect of grammar. Or if your teacher marks a piece of your work and tells you that you are making certain errors, you could work, in your own time, through the material that will help you use and understand that particular grammar feature. This could be especially helpful when you are writing or redrafting coursework that will be sent away as part of an exam course.

However, you do not have to be a school or college learner to use this book. It is designed to make sense to anyone using, or learning to use, English grammar and language. You could **work through the book in your own time** from start to finish, or you could pick out the chapters and sections that you think would be most helpful.

The design of the book will support you as you work through the material.

When a new piece of key knowledge or a new rule is introduced, it will look like this:

> This box contains information that is very important: it is something you will want to remember.

It will be useful to access the information in these boxes even when you do not have this book beside you. So, here are two suggestions:

➤ You could copy out the boxed information into a certain place. It could all go together at the back of your English jotter or in a special notebook you keep just for that purpose.

➤ You could take a photo of the information box and store all the pictures together in a 'grammar' album on your phone or tablet.

In some parts of the book, you will see these headings being used:

 Building

 Strengthening

 Extending

These tell you that the work you are doing is becoming more challenging and that you are truly increasing your knowledge and skills.

Crossover

This box shows where your knowledge and skills cross over. For example, you will learn about using capital letters to start sentences, but you will also learn to use them in proper nouns.

Mistake!

This box shows mistakes that some writers make but which you can easily learn to avoid.

And when you come across a page beginning like this:

Bringing it all together

it will introduce a revision task at an appropriate point in the book that will let you test yourself on what you have been learning up to that point. These tasks are very useful for **homework** if you are using the book at school. 'Bringing it all together' pages may be **photocopied**.

Answers to all tasks throughout the book can be found online at www.hoddergibson.co.uk/answers-grammar. If you have any problems accessing the answers document online, you can contact hoddergibson@hodder.co.uk to get an email version sent to you.

Why grammar matters

▶ What is grammar?

Grammar is the collection of rules and guidelines that we follow when we use and structure our language. Grammar can be made of incredibly small things. A **full stop** is just a tiny dot on a page. Good grammar can be about understanding something as small as the difference between two **punctuation marks**, such as ; and :

If the differences are so small, why does grammar matter?

Grammar matters because it helps us to write what we mean and to mean what we write. If your grammar is wrong, you will not be able to make your meaning clear. People who read your writing might think you are saying something that you did not actually intend, or they might not understand you at all.

Let me prove my point. Look at this sentence:

The girls like ice cream.

It tells us that a number of young female people enjoy eating a cold creamy food that often comes in a cone. However, if you use an **apostrophe** where you shouldn't, you get this:

The girl's like ice cream.

which creates a very unfortunate impression.

Here are two sentences that use all the same letters in the same order. Only the **punctuation** has changed. How would each sentence make the grandfather feel? Can you explain the very worrying idea that is suggested in the second sentence?

Let's eat, Grandpa.   Let's eat Grandpa!

Now look at this example:

I'm sorry I love you.

This short sentence tells us that I regret loving you – in fact, I'd really rather I *didn't* feel this way!

Look what happens if we use exactly the same words in exactly the same order, but just change the grammar and punctuation.

> I'm sorry; I love you.

Can you explain what the sentence means this time? It might help if you read it out loud or get your teacher to do so if you are using this book in school.

Look at the following two examples. Can you see the difference?

> This is Andrew. Who could be more attractive?

> This is Andrew, who could be more attractive.

Group task

You will see two letters. Each one contains exactly the same words in the same order. Only the **punctuation** is different, but this totally changes the meaning. Half the pupils in your class should practise reading the first version out loud; the other half should practise the second version. Be as expressive as possible. When you're ready, one person from each half of the class should read their version aloud.

Dear Jack

I want a man who knows what love is all about. You are generous, kind, thoughtful. People who are not like you admit to being useless and inferior. You have ruined me for other men. I yearn for you. I have no feelings whatsoever when we're apart. I can be forever happy – will you let me be yours?

Jill

Dear Jack

I want a man who knows what love is. All about you are generous, kind, thoughtful people, who are not like you. Admit to being useless and inferior. You have ruined me. For other men I yearn! For you I have no feelings whatsoever. When we're apart I can be forever happy. Will you let me be?

Yours,

Jill

I hope you can see now that grammar is vital because good grammar creates clear communication. This is important in your English lessons at school where you will probably do most of your learning about grammar. But, using good grammar matters in every other subject too. It matters when you write your coursework for **all** your exam subjects and when you sit the exams themselves, because you can't earn marks for something the examiner can't understand. Grammar is important when you write a job application or send a complaint email or give a presentation at work.

Grammar matters because grammar makes meaning.

1 Parts of speech

Different words have different jobs to do. Look at this sentence:

> The brum tublup was dinating gurdly beside the condle pirrostin.

Don't worry if the sentence seems like nonsense. You should still be able to answer these questions about it.

1   What was the tublup like?
2   What was the tublup doing?
3   How did the tublup do this?
4   What was the pirrostin like?

If you find those questions really tricky, you could think of it like this:

> The brum tublup was dinating gurdly beside the condle pirrostin.

is organised in exactly the same way, with the same structure, as this sentence:

> The old dog was dreaming quietly beside the warm radiator.

Now try again to answer those four questions.

You could work out the correct answers for these questions because you can already speak and write English. You already have a wide and deep knowledge of how our language works. This chapter about parts of speech – like many other chapters in this book – will give you a way to understand, handle and discuss this knowledge. That knowledge will also be stretched, added to and challenged.

The expression **parts of speech** means the different sorts of words that we have in the English language and the different jobs that those words do for us. The main English parts of speech are:

nouns	adverbs	conjunctions
adjectives	pronouns	articles
verbs	prepositions	interjections

▶ Nouns

You most likely used your first ever spoken word when you were about a year old and that word was probably a **noun**. You might have used the name of someone in your family. You might have said the word for your favourite toy or a family pet. All of those words are nouns. If we can use nouns then we can start, at least in a simple way, to talk about the world around us. For example, if a baby can say 'banana', someone can give the baby a chunk of that fruit; if a baby can say 'teddy', someone can give the baby a cuddly toy.

> A **noun** is a naming word. It tells us the name of a thing, place or person. Nouns are the words that help us to identify and talk about what we find in the world around us.

There are several different types of noun. We are going to start with the simplest and most common type. In fact, there is a clue in the name.

›› Common nouns

> A **common noun** is a word that tells us the name of a thing we can experience with our senses. Common nouns are the names of things that we can see, hear and touch. It can be helpful if we think of common nouns as the names of ordinary things:
>
> | | | |
> |---|---|---|
> | dog | gate | biscuit |
> | hat | train | leaf |

 Group task

Take a few seconds to look around the room you are in. Everyone in your group or class should then take it in turns to say the **common noun** for something they can see from where they are sitting. Make sure you listen carefully so that you don't say a common noun someone has said already.

If your group is quite small, or if you are in a big class but ready for a challenge, keep going round and round until nobody can see any more common nouns.

Building

Read the following extract. It contains **23** different **common nouns**. Can you find them all?

> The café was packed. A barista at the counter was energetically pulling the lever on a vast, shiny machine, skilfully turning out cup after cup of steaming coffee. A speedy waiter slipped quickly between the tables, delivering plates of cake and bowls of spicy-smelling soup. In the corner, by the window, sat a small woman, quietly tapping away at the keys of a shiny laptop. She ignored everything around her, until she was disturbed by a sudden bark. An unsupervised toddler had pulled a dog's ears. The woman smiled sympathetically at the dog, scowled at the child and went back to whatever she was thinking about.

|H|H| **Strengthening**

The paragraph above describes a busy café. How many more **common nouns** can you think of for things that could be found in that café scene? Make a list.

 Extending

So far you have identified common nouns in someone else's writing or made lists of common nouns. Now it is time to use some common nouns in your own writing.

First, pick **one** of the following locations. Make a list of at least **ten common nouns** for things you would expect to find there:

➤ a supermarket   ➤ a street in town   ➤ a museum   ➤ a sports ground

Next, write about **100 words** to describe the scene in that place. Use all the common nouns from your list. HINT! It may help if you look back at the café scene paragraph on page 3, which was just over 100 words long.

Finally, read back over your writing. Underline all the common nouns as you go. Did you use all the common nouns on your list? Did you use any others as well?

There are several different types of noun. We have started with the simplest and most frequent type, the common noun, and you have practised identifying these and knowing where to use them. Let's move on to the next kind of noun.

>> Proper nouns

A **proper noun** is the name of a particular person or place:

Tom Hanks	New York	Kings Cross Station
Beyoncé	Germany	Loch Ness

Proper nouns **always** begin with a **capital letter**.

 Building

Read the following extract. It contains **15** different **proper nouns**. Can you find them all? HINT! Some of the proper nouns here are made up of more than one word.

It took Romesh and Claire a long time to plan their holiday. At first, they thought they might go to France. Paris would be lovely at this time of year, and they could climb the Eiffel Tower or take a boat along the Seine at night. Then they considered Germany. Berlin would be a fascinating city to visit, and they could stay with Claire's Aunt Frida, who lived very near the Brandenburg Gate. Romesh really wanted to take Claire to Sri Lanka, to see where his family had come from, but it was too far away, and it would cost too much money. At last, they decided to spend a weekend in London: the only language they both knew how to speak was English, and the British Museum and the National Gallery would both be free.

Strengthening – group task

Get everybody in your group or class to stand up. Everyone has a name, which is a proper noun. Take a few seconds to look around the room. When you all feel ready, the person whose **first name** comes nearest to the start of the alphabet should say their name out loud and then sit down. The person whose name comes second should say theirs and then sit down. Carry on around the class until everyone is sitting down.

To extend the challenge, get everyone to stand up and play the game again, but this time use everyone's **surname** alphabetically.

⤬ Crossover

As you do the next few tasks, remember that proper nouns **always** begin with a capital letter. That is not the only reason why we use capital letters in English. We also use them at the beginning of sentences, which you can learn about on page 115.

Building

The word 'country' is a common noun because there are lots of countries in the world. But in the example above, France, Germany and Sri Lanka are the names of particular countries. They are proper nouns and they start with capital letters.

Look at the table on the next page. The middle column is full of **common nouns**. The left column lists the **proper nouns** that go with those common nouns – just as 'Germany' goes with 'country' or 'Romesh' goes with 'man'. But the proper nouns in the first column are in the wrong order. Match each common noun with the correct proper noun. One has been done for you as an example.

Proper noun	Common noun	Proper noun
India	island	
Aisha	continent	
Europe	company	
Tuesday	country	
September	river	
Tasmania	girl	
Islam	building	
Amazon	language	
Pacific	month	
Polish	mountain	Ben Nevis
Mount Everest	religion	
Nike	state	
Texas	ocean	
Houses of Parliament	day	

 ## Strengthening

Now look at the empty third column of the table. Find another **proper noun** to go alongside each of the common nouns in the middle column. For example, 'Ben Nevis' is a proper noun that goes with 'mountain'.

Extending

You learned already that proper nouns are the names of particular people or places. We can see that in the table above. Girls are people. Buildings, continents, countries, islands, mountains, oceans, rivers and states are all different sorts of places.

But there are some other, quite specific, reasons why we use proper nouns. They are not used only for names of people and places. What **other types of proper noun** can you find in the table above?

You already know about common nouns and proper nouns. Let's move on to another kind of noun.

❯❯ Abstract nouns

An **abstract noun** is the name of an emotion, an idea, a value or a quality:

anger	belief	bravery
love	kindness	patience

We know that these things are real: they are important to us and they affect our thoughts and feelings. We understand them. However, unlike common nouns, we can't see them or touch them and, unlike proper nouns, we can't meet them or visit them.

In the box above, 'anger' and 'love' are abstract nouns that name **emotions**. Make a list of all the other emotions you can think of.

'Kindness' and 'bravery' are abstract nouns that name personal **qualities**. Make a list of all the other qualities you can think of.

 Group task

One by one, get people in your class to read out their lists of **emotions**. Listen carefully. Every time you hear someone else say an emotion that is also on your list, tick it off. Once everyone has read their lists, look to see if you have any abstract nouns left that nobody else thought of. How many? Does anyone else still have more than you?

Now do the same with your lists of personal qualities.

You have now learned about three types of nouns: common nouns, proper nouns and abstract nouns. There's just one more type to go.

❯❯ Collective nouns

A **collective noun** is the name for a group or collection of similar people, animals or things:

a pack of cards	a flock of sheep	a class of pupils

1 Parts of speech

Building

What is the **collective noun** for the following?

1 singers	2 grapes	3 cows
4 fish	5 birds	6 bees
7 people in a church or other religious building	8 people in a theatre or at a concert	
9 people who play a sport together	10 a family of baby kittens or puppies	

Strengthening

These are much more unusual – you may need to research them online. What is the **collective noun** for the following?

11 owls   12 crows   13 lions   14 locusts

Extending

In a competition to make up new collective nouns a few years ago, one of the winning entries was:

a barcode of zebras

Can you explain why this is a good suggestion?

So far in this chapter, you have learned about the four main types of noun. You know how to tell a common noun from a proper noun; you also know about abstract nouns and collective nouns. You are now ready to move on and learn about a different kind of word – one that always goes with a noun.

▶ Adjectives

You have already learned about nouns – the words that give names to things. Once we can name things we can start to talk about the world. But the things around us are varied and different. Adjectives help us to talk about those differences. Adjectives help us to **describe** things and to think, speak and write in detail.

An **adjective** is a describing word. It tells us what a noun is like. An adjective **adds** something to a noun. (Thinking of the word 'add' can help us remember this.)

a blue car   a friendly dog   a tall woman   an infectious illness

Building

Read the following extract, which you have seen before. As well as the nouns you have already found, it contains **nine** different **adjectives**. Can you find them all?

The café was packed. A barista at the counter was energetically pulling the lever on a vast, shiny machine, skilfully turning out cup after cup of steaming coffee. A speedy waiter slipped quickly between the tables, delivering plates of cake and bowls of spicy-smelling soup. In the corner, by the window, sat a small woman, quietly tapping away at the keys of a shiny laptop. She ignored everything around her, until she was disturbed by a sudden bark. An unsupervised toddler had pulled a dog's ears. The woman smiled sympathetically at the dog, scowled at the child and went back to whatever she was thinking about.

Strengthening – group task

Take a few seconds to look around the room you are in. Everyone in your group or class should then take it in turns to say an **adjective** that describes something they can see from where they are sitting. Other members of your class should then try to guess the noun from the adjective.

For example, if one person says the adjective 'blue', which describes the colour of something, another person might guess that it is the blue poster on the wall or one of the blue desks in the classroom. Your teacher will listen to make sure that all the words given really are correct adjectives.

Extending

Read the following sentences. In each sentence, pick out the **adjectives** and identify the **nouns** that they tell us about. The first one has been done for you as an example.

1   A wild wind whipped through the trees and whirled dead leaves across the empty park.

Adjective: wild	*Noun: wind*
Adjective: dead	*Noun: leaves*
Adjective: empty	*Noun: park*

2   She meant to buy herself some new football boots but came home with a warm blue jacket instead.

3   The grumpy driver muttered under her breath as the crammed bus crept through the heavy traffic.

4   The fascinated audience were so gripped by the complicated plot of the play that it took a few seconds for them to move when the theatre's shrill fire alarm went off.

5   His meal didn't look very tasty. The steak was burnt and the shrivelled lettuce leaf beside it on the cracked plate didn't really live up to the green salad the tempting menu had promised.

6   Using the scrubby bushes as camouflage, the ageing lioness crept up on the elegant giraffe.

So far you have identified adjectives in someone else's writing. Now it is time to think of adjectives that you could use in your own writing.

Building

Make a list of all the **adjectives** you can think of that would describe:

➤ a kitten   ➤ a criminal   ➤ a clown   ➤ a spaceship

➤ a crocodile   ➤ a pop star   ➤ a monster   ➤ a cloud

Try to think of **at least five** possible adjectives for each noun.

Strengthening

Some adjectives are so overused that they have become weak: they don't really say anything interesting or worthwhile. In your own writing you should try to use adjectives that really feel as if they are telling us something useful or interesting about the nouns.

Read the following passage. The weak, worn-out adjectives have been picked out in **blue**. For each one, choose a more interesting and precise adjective to take its place. HINT! Think carefully about which word would be best for the story that the passage is telling.

There was almost a **(1) big** crash on the high street yesterday, just next to the **(2) little** shop that sells those **(3) nice** cakes. The baker was just putting some **(4) new** pastries in the window when she spotted a **(5) fast** car coming up the road. At that **(6) important** moment, a lorry pulled away from the curb. I don't think either of the drivers was looking, which is a really **(7) bad** way to behave on any street, especially one as busy as this.

The man in the car couldn't see up the road past the **(8) big** lorry. He slammed on his brakes and screeched to a halt, right in front of a **(9) little (10) old** lady who was about to cross the road. I'm **(11) happy** to say that she wasn't hurt, but she did get a **(12) bad** fright.

The lorry drove away – I don't think the driver even realised what had happened. The car driver behaved better. He apologised to the lady, and took her into the shop where he bought her a cake and a **(13) nice** cup of tea. That was **(14) good** of him, but he needs to slow down in town.

By the way, there were **two** other adjectives in the passage. Did you spot them?

 Extending

Look at this picture.

Write a description of the place. Use interesting, well-chosen **adjectives** as you write. HINT! It may help if you look back at the café scene paragraph on page 3.

Then, read back over your writing. Underline all the adjectives as you go. How many did you manage to use?

It's time now to add a bit more detail to your understanding of adjectives.

You understand already that adjectives are describing words and that they tell us about **nouns**. So far we have looked at how they describe **common nouns**. But adjectives can also be used to describe our experience of feelings and emotions, which, as you learned already, are **abstract nouns**.

Complete the tables to show which adjectives go with which abstract nouns. The first one in each table has been done for you as an example.

Adjective	Abstract noun
angry	anger
	shame
frustrated	
annoyed	
	anxiety
sad	
	excitement

Adjective	Abstract noun
happy	happiness
sorry	
	disgust
embarrassed	
	jealousy
	fear
fascinated	

›› Comparative and superlative adjectives

So far we have used adjectives to say what a noun is like or to say what someone feels like. Adjectives can do more for us than that. They can tell us what someone or something is like **compared to** someone or something else. We call these **comparative** and **superlative adjectives**.

A **comparative adjective** lets us compare one thing, or one person, to another:

Marcus is **taller** than Omar.   Kemi is **older** than Meera.

A **superlative adjective** tells us that something is the most or best that it can be:

the **tallest** man   the **oldest** woman

We find the -st ending of the words 'most' and 'best' in many superlative adjectives, which is one way that we can spot them.

Group task

This will take a few minutes to organise. Get everyone in your group or class to find two different examples of the same sort of object – for example, two books or two pencils.

When you are all ready, each person should show the class their two chosen objects and say something about them using a **comparative adjective**. For example:

The blue pencil is **sharper** than the yellow one.

Carry on around the class until everyone has spoken. If someone gets stuck and cannot think how to compare their two objects, they can show them to the teacher who will think of a comparison for them.

Building

The simplest way to make a comparative adjective in English is by adding -er to the end of the word. The simplest way of making a superlative adjective is by adding -est to the basic adjective. Complete these **adjectives**.

Descriptive	Comparative	Superlative
tall		
rich		
old		
light		
kind		

Strengthening

If you are adding -er or -est to an adjective that ends in -y, you have to change the -y to an -i-. You can see an example of this in the first row of the table below. Complete the **adjectives** in the table on the next page.

Descriptive	Comparative	Superlative
frilly	frillier	frilliest
wobbly		
crazy		
hairy		
shabby		
grumpy		

If you are adding -er or -est to an adjective that is only one syllable long and has a short vowel sound in it, you usually need to double the final consonant before you add the -er or -est ending. You can see an example in the first row of the table below.

 Crossover

You can learn more about **vowels** and **consonants** on page 133.

Complete these adjectives.

Descriptive	Comparative	Superlative
fat	fatter	fattest
big		
wet		
sad		
hot		
thin		

Some adjectives just don't sound right if we try to use any of the above rules to make comparatives or superlatives. For example, we would never say or write:

excitinger   beautifulest

For these adjectives, we create comparatives by using 'more', and we create superlatives by using 'most':

more exciting   most beautiful

 Extending

Using all the rules and advice you have just learned, complete these **adjectives**.

Descriptive	Comparative	Superlative
shiny		
popular		
clever		
wonderful		
long		
silly		
small		
clumsy		
cheerful		
lonely		
heavy		
important		
slim		
dry		
sharp		
ugly		

There are some adjectives that don't follow any of these rules for making comparatives and superlatives. They are totally irregular, and you just have to know them. For example:

bad – worse – worst   good – better – best   many – more – most   little – less – least

If you have grown up speaking English, you know these already without even realising that you do.

Finally, some adjectives can't be compared at all. A 'daily' event can't happen 'dailier'. An 'innocent' person cannot be 'innocenter'. There are lots of adjectives like this.

Now that you know how to spell and build comparative and superlative adjectives, let's think a bit more about how to use them.

You use a comparative adjective when you are talking or writing about **two** things:

Madeleine is the **younger** of Rachel's two children.

The blue car is **dirtier** than the black one.

You use a superlative adjective when you are talking or writing about **three or more** things:

Sam is the **youngest** of Michael's four children.

The white car was the **dirtiest** of all the ones for sale on the garage forecourt.

Using the prompts below to help you, make sentences using comparative or superlative adjectives. Make your sentences as interesting as possible by using a varied vocabulary. One has been done for you as an example.

1   many kinds of dinosaur (vicious)

As we have learned from a number of famous films, of all the many dinosaurs that ever roamed the Earth, the Velociraptor was the most vicious.

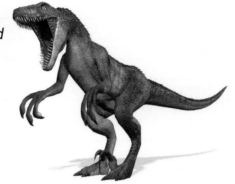

2   two suitcases (heavy)

3   a pile of books (long)

4   two diamonds (sharp)

5   a platoon of soldiers (fit)

6   all the songs in the chart (loud)

7   two shades of grey paint (dull)

8   four tables in an antique shop (old and scratched)

To end our work on adjectives, here are two warnings that will help you to write better.

> ## Mistake!
> Adjectives are wonderful words. They bring detail and description into our use of language. But you don't have to send every noun out into the world with an adjective to keep it company. Nouns don't get lonely without an adjective to look after them. Using too many adjectives can be like putting too much icing on your cupcake – in the end, it gets overpowering. Read this to see what I mean:
>
> **The hairy little dog ran round the vibrant green lawn yapping at the round rubber ball its adoring young owner threw for it.**

> ## Mistake!
> Some adjectives and nouns don't need to go together because the noun already suggests the idea in the adjective. A scream is always shrill and the sound of a whistle is always piercing, so there is no need to write about 'a shrill scream' or 'a piercing whistle'. You should only use adjectives when they add something to the noun.

> ### ⤭ Crossover
> You will find similar advice about overuse and unnecessary use when you learn about **adverbs** on page 28.

Bringing it all together

▶ Nouns and adjectives

Now that you have learned about nouns and the adjectives that often go with them, you are ready to revise and check your learning.

You learned that there are four types of noun.

Answer these questions about nouns.

1   a   What do we call nouns like 'snow', 'builder', 'traffic light' and 'packet'?

   b   Add four more nouns of this type to the list above.

2   a   What do we call nouns like 'Sam', 'Sydney Harbour Bridge' and 'Rome'?

   b   Add four more nouns of this type to the list above.

   c   What must you always do when you write down this type of noun?

3   a   What do we call nouns like 'love', 'care', 'fear', 'help' and 'confidence'?

   b   Add four more nouns of this type to the list above.

4   a   What do we call nouns like 'group' and 'shoal'?

   b   Add two more nouns of this type to the list above.

Answer these questions about adjectives.

5   a   Write a brief explanation of what an adjective is and what it does.

   b   Make a list of four adjectives.

6   a   Write a brief explanation of what a comparative adjective is and what it does.

   b   Make a list of four comparative adjectives.

7   a   Write a brief explanation of what a superlative adjective is and what it does.

   b   Make a list of four superlative adjectives.

▶ Verbs

We learned earlier that your first spoken word was probably a noun – a word that names something. Some of your other early words were probably **verbs**. If we can use verbs, then we can start to make simple sentences. If a baby can say 'Want teddy', someone can look for the baby's favourite bear; if a baby can say 'Go park', someone can take the baby to that special place.

> A **verb** is a doing word. It tells us about action:
>
> skate   write   clamber   walk   pour   drop
>
> Verbs can also tell us about being and having:
>
> It **is** freezing today.   I **have** a nasty cold.
>
> **HINT!** The verb of being can be very tricky to spot.
>
> Verbs can also tell us about feelings:
>
> I believe   she loves   you hate
>
> Verbs are very important because we need a verb to make a proper sentence:
>
> To the park. ×   He **took** the baby to the park. ✓
>
> In a sentence, the person or thing that does the verb is called the **subject** of the sentence.

 Group task

Everyone in your group or class should take it in turns to say a verb for something that you think most people do every day. Make sure you listen carefully so that you don't say a verb someone has said already.

 Building

Find the **verbs** in the following sentences.

1   Samira won a sports scholarship to an excellent university.

2   John's grandparents live near a beach.

3   The passengers sighed with relief as the plane skidded to a halt.

4   A TV murmured quietly in the corner of the room.

5 The Post Office van idled at the traffic lights.

6 A bell rang and hundreds of pupils moved from class to class.

Strengthening

Read the following extract, which you have seen before. It uses **14** different **verbs**. Can you find them all? This task is much trickier than the similar ones you did when you looked for nouns and adjectives in this café scene. HINT! Remember that the verb of being can be tricky to spot.

> The café was packed. A barista at the counter was energetically pulling the lever on a vast, shiny machine, skilfully turning out cup after cup of steaming coffee. A speedy waiter slipped quickly between the tables, delivering plates of cake and bowls of spicy-smelling soup. In the corner, by the window, sat a small woman, quietly tapping away at the keys of a shiny laptop. She ignored everything around her, until she was disturbed by a sudden bark. An unsupervised toddler had pulled a dog's ears. The woman smiled sympathetically at the dog, scowled at the child and went back to whatever she was thinking about.

So far you have identified verbs in someone else's writing. Now it is time to use some verbs of your own.

Building

Certain nouns suggest certain verbs. Fish swim. Birds fly. Dogs wag their tails. For each of the following nouns, suggest a **verb** that goes with it.

➤ bees   ➤ rats   ➤ authors   ➤ bells

➤ ice   ➤ diamonds   ➤ pilots   ➤ mountaineers

Strengthening

Choose a suitable **verb** to complete each sentence. There are lots of possibilities, so think carefully about interesting words you could use.

1 The home team _____ the match.

2 Parents _____ the best for their children.

3 Her nephew _____ the guitar.

4 The car _____ the lamp post.

5 David _____ over the fence.

6 That exam really _____ all the students who sat it.

Extending

Now, pick **one** of these characters:

➤ a thief   ➤ a police officer   ➤ a newspaper reporter

and **one** of these locations:

➤ a supermarket   ➤ a street in town   ➤ a museum

Next, write about **100 words** about that character in that place. Just describe what the character is doing, or did, there. You can decide to write it in the present tense, as if it is happening now, or in the past tense, as if it has happened already. (You will learn more about tenses very soon.) HINT! If you feel a bit stuck and are not sure how to start, this picture might help you.

Now, read back over your writing. Underline all the verbs as you go. HINT! Look out for those verbs of being. How many verbs did you use?

Finally, if you are doing this task in a class, swap your work with someone else. Check if they spotted all their verbs. Underline any more verbs that you notice (using a wiggly line to make them stand out).

Now that you have practised identifying verbs and using them, you are ready to learn about the more complex aspects of this part of speech.

❯❯ Tenses

You already know that verbs are doing words. They tell us about an action – about something happening. Every verb also tells us **when** that action or event happens.

The **tense** adds the idea of time to a verb. Tenses let us know if something happened in the **past**:

>I **learned** to play tennis when I was just a kid.

or is happening now in the **present**:

>My mum **is playing** tennis with her friend.

or will happen in the **future**:

>I **will have** more time for tennis after I retire.

Building

Read the following sentences. Decide if each once is in the **past**, **present** or **future** tense. **HINT!** Keep watching out for that sneaky verb of being.

1 I run along the canal to get to work.

2 I am running a marathon later this year to raise money for charity.

3 I ran a small coffee stall beside the swings in the park.

4 I am running towards you right this minute.

5 I have been to London quite a few times.

6 I had been in London earlier that year.

7 I will be in London just before Christmas.

8 I hated living in London.

9 I hate black coffee: it tastes metallic and oily.

10 I am going to open a coffee shop in that quiet part of London by Regent's Canal.

11 I will open a new jar of coffee when this one is empty.

12 I can't talk to you now: I'm trying to open the coffee jar, but the lid is stuck.

Strengthening

1 Using the **past tense**, write **five** sentences that each have the word 'yesterday' in them. When you have written your sentences, go back and underline the verbs.

2 Using the **present tense**, write **five** sentences that each have the word 'now' in them. When you have written your sentences, go back and underline the verbs.

3 Using the **future tense**, write **five** sentences that each have the word 'tomorrow' in them. When you have written your sentences, go back and underline the verbs.

Extending

The following passage is in the past tense. Re-write it to put it into the **present tense**.

I lived in Venice for three years. Every morning I sauntered along the Grand Canal until I reached the Rialto Bridge. I walked under the last span of the bridge and turned left into the market. It was full of stalls that sold fish, fruit, vegetables and all sorts of bread and cakes. I wandered up and down until I found something tasty for my lunch. Then I bought a tiny, very strong coffee from a nearby café and sat by the waterside drinking it and watching the world go by.

The following passage is in the present tense. Re-write it to put it into the **past tense**.

> On Tuesday and Thursday afternoons I go to my language class. The teacher is a very strict woman who often tells me off for not sounding like a real Italian. She says I should practise more by talking to the stallholders every morning. She gets annoyed with me because she knows I just point at what I want in the market and hold up my wallet when I want to know the price. She makes me practise my accent by reading out sentences from a children's story about a cat.

You know now that tenses inform us if something happened in the past, is happening now in the present or will happen in the future. But they are a little more complex and cleverer than that.

The way that we build past tense verbs can tell us how far back in the past something happened. Using 'had' as part of the verb pushes the action further back into the past.

> I had been to London five times before I got the chance to visit the famous zoo and see the penguins.

suggests that the first five visits to London happened before visit number six, when the speaker finally went to the zoo.

> She had hit the ball so hard that it flew right out over the top of the stadium.

suggests that the hitting happened before the ball's exit from the stadium: without the hitting, the ball would not have flown so far.

The way that we build present tense verbs can tell us if something is happening right now or happens more generally.

> I am singing along to the music in my earbuds.

tells us that this person is singing right now at this very moment.

> I sing in a choir that meets in the community centre.

tells us that this person sings regularly as a habit.

There are two ways to build future tense verbs. The easiest way is to use 'will'.

> You will use your knowledge of grammar in your English coursework.

> That cake will be ready in about half an hour.

But we also often use the phrase 'going to' – which sounds like the present tense – to talk or write about future actions.

I am going to scream if that phone rings again.

She's going to visit her granny next Saturday.

Understanding the idea of tense will help you to grasp the next part of our knowledge of verbs.

>> Regular and irregular verbs

Some verbs are **regular**. They follow a pattern, do what we expect and behave themselves. Some verbs are **irregular**. They keep changing and don't seem to follow a rule. We often notice that a verb is irregular when we look at its past tense.

Regular verbs just add -ed or -d to make the past tense. For example:

➤ shout – shouted   ➤ smile – smiled

➤ ask – asked   ➤ work – worked

The past tenses of some irregular verbs are still quite closely related to their present tense. The spelling of the past tense is different but not very different. For example:

➤ sing – sang   ➤ swim – swam   ➤ run – ran   ➤ write – wrote

Some irregular verbs have past tenses that are very different from their present tenses. The two verbs we use most often in English are very irregular. Here is the verb of going:

➤ Present tense: I/you/they go   he/she/it goes

➤ Past tense: I/you/they/he/she/it went

Here is the verb of being:

➤ Present tense: I am   you/they are   he/she/it is

➤ Past tense: I was   you/they were   he/she/it was

That might all seem very strange and complicated. Don't panic! First of all, you can always look back to these pages of the book if you ever need a reminder about regular and irregular verbs. More important, although it is interesting to know that some verbs are regular and some are irregular, you actually don't have to learn them. If you have grown up speaking English, you will know these already without even realising that you do.

Do this task to prove to yourself that you can easily cope with regular and irregular verbs.

1   You saw above that 'shout', 'ask', 'smile' and 'work' are regular verbs, with past tenses that end in -d or -ed. Make a list of **five** more regular verbs.

2   You saw above that 'sing', 'run', 'swim' and 'write' are slightly irregular verbs. Make a list of **three** more verbs that are a little bit irregular with their spelling changing slightly in the past tense.

3   In the explanation on the previous page, the verb of going was organised into three groups to help you understand it.

   a   Write a sentence that uses any option from the 'go' group.

   b   Write a sentence that uses any option from the 'goes' group.

   c   Write a sentence that uses any option from the 'went' group.

4   In the explanation on the previous page, the verb of being was organised into six groups to help you understand it.

   a   Write a sentence that includes 'I am'.

   b   Write a sentence that includes 'you are' or 'they are'.

   c   Write a sentence that includes 'he is', 'she is' or 'it is'.

   d   Write a sentence that includes 'I was'.

   e   Write a sentence that includes 'you were' or 'they were'.

   f   Write a sentence that includes 'he was', 'she was' or 'it was'.

We still have two more things to learn about verbs. We are going to learn about infinitives and about intransitive and transitive verbs. If you can master these, you will understand and be able to explain things that many adult users of English are not able to explain (even though these things are not difficult to understand). Also, if you have the understanding and the vocabulary to discuss them, you will be able to use that knowledge in any English exams you sit when you are older.

›› Infinitives

> The **infinitive** is the basic form of the verb. English infinitives are always made of **two words**, and the first word is always 'to':
>
> to be   to have   to run   to go   to want   to hide

The infinitive is the most basic form of the verb. It doesn't tell us anything about time, because it has no tense: we don't know when the running or hiding happens. Infinitives also don't tell us anything about person: we don't know who wants or who goes or who has.

Group task

Everyone in your group or class should take it in turns to say an **infinitive verb**. Don't use any of the six you see in the box above: there are thousands of infinitives in English! Make sure you listen carefully so that you don't say a verb someone has said already.

›› Intransitive and transitive verbs

> **Intransitive verbs** just happen:
>
> She **runs** to work each day.   He **speaks** very loudly.

Transitive verbs are done **to** something or someone. That something or someone is the **object** of the verb:

She **runs** a small business.   The detective **found** a clue at the scene.

As you can see with 'runs' in the boxes above, some verbs can be either intransitive or transitive depending on what else we find in the sentence. But some verbs are only one kind or the other.

One good reason for knowing about transitive and intransitive verbs is to stop you confusing some verbs that lots of people mix up. Look at these cartoons and sentences.

My arm was itching.

I scratched it far too hard.

Ms Cooper enjoyed teaching us.

We learned so much.

I had to lie down for a rest.

He laid out the playing cards.

Which are the intransitive verbs? Can you put each one into its infinitive form?

Which are the transitive verbs? Can you put each one into its infinitive form?

These pairs of transitive and intransitive verbs often get mixed up, but now you know how to avoid that mistake.

So far in this chapter you have learned about verbs. You know that verbs have a tense, which tells us when the verb happens. You have learned that some verbs are regular while others are irregular, you know about the infinitive form of verbs and you know the difference between intransitive and transitive verbs.

You are now ready to move on and learn about a different kind of word – one that goes with a verb.

▶ Adverbs

You have already learned about verbs – the words that tell us about doing. But different people might do the same things in different ways. Adverbs help us to talk and write about those differences.

> An adverb – as you can easily see from the word itself – **adds** something to a verb. An adverb tells us **how** a verb is done:
>
> He sings **badly**, but she sings very **well**.
>
> Trees grow **slowly**, but crops like potatoes and corn grow much more **quickly**.

The words 'badly' and 'well' tell us how the two people sing. The words 'slowly' and 'quickly' tell us how the crops grow.

Many adverbs end in -ly, which is a clue that can help you to spot them.

Building

Read the following extract, which you have seen before. As well as the nouns, adjectives and verbs you have already found, it also contains **five** different **adverbs**. Can you find them all? For each adverb that you find, say which verb it goes with.

The café was packed. A barista at the counter was energetically pulling the lever on a vast, shiny machine, skilfully turning out cup after cup of steaming coffee. A speedy waiter slipped quickly between the tables, delivering plates of cake and bowls of spicy-smelling soup. In the corner, by the window, sat a small woman, quietly tapping away at the keys of a shiny laptop. She ignored everything around her, until she was disturbed by a sudden bark. An unsupervised toddler had pulled a dog's ears. The woman smiled sympathetically at the dog, scowled at the child and went back to whatever she was thinking about.

Strengthening

First, pick at least **five** of these adjectives. Add -ly to each one to turn it into an **adverb**.

- quiet
- loud
- rude
- clear
- beautiful
- careful
- soft
- kind
- safe
- light

Then, use each **adverb** in a sentence. Choose the most interesting words and ideas that you can as you create those sentences.

Sometimes we need to change the adjective a little before we can add -ly to make it into an adverb.

If the adjective ends in -y, we change that -y to an -i- before adding the -ly. For example:

lucky – luckily   hungry – hungrily

If the adjective ends in -e, we drop that -e before adding the -ly. For example:

sensible – sensibly   terrible – terribly

Extending

First, pick at least **six** of these adjectives. Add -ly to each one and make the other spelling changes needed to turn it into an **adverb**. Look at the spelling advice on the previous page if you need to.

> greedy   > true   > angry   > happy

> noisy   > busy   > gentle   > easy

Then, use each adverb in a sentence. Choose the most interesting words and ideas that you can as you create those sentences.

You know now that adverbs tell us **how** a verb is done. It's time to learn what else they can do for us.

Adverbs can also let us know:

When an action happens:

We received the parcel **yesterday**.

Where an action happens:

Come **here** and bring me that book.

How much or **how often** an action happens:

Sometimes he stays with his dad; **sometimes** he is at his mum's.

 Building

Make three columns in your notebook. Call the first column **WHEN?**, the second column **WHERE?** and the third column **HOW MUCH?**

Look at this list of adverbs. At the moment they are in alphabetical order. Sort them into the correct columns in your notebook to show what each adverb tells us about the verb or action.

- above
- almost
- already
- before
- behind
- completely
- everywhere
- hardly
- here
- immediately
- in
- less
- now
- nowhere
- often
- out
- outside
- quite
- since
- so
- soon
- there
- today
- tomorrow
- very
- yesterday

·I⊢I· Strengthening – group task

There are other **adverbs** that you could add to each of those three columns. Can you think of any? Add them to your notebook. If you are working in a class or group, you could do this task together to gather more ideas. Make sure you write down every good answer you hear.

Adverbs are wonderful words. They bring detail and description into our use of language. Because we have adverbs, we can write:

> 'I don't know what you mean,' she said nastily.

instead of something much clumsier like:

> 'I don't know what you mean,' she said with a nasty tone in her voice.

There are, however, **three** mistakes that are often made with adverbs. Learning about these will help you to write better.

> ## Mistake!
> You don't have to send every verb out into the world with an adverb to keep it company. You can often miss out a 'how' adverb altogether by choosing an interesting and expressive verb.
>
> For example, instead of writing:
>
> **He walked unsteadily.**
>
> you could use a more interesting and expressive **verb** and write:
>
> **He stumbled.**

Instead of writing:

The tiny creature ran lightly across the room.

you could write:

The tiny creature scampered across the room.

if you want your readers to like the beastie, or:

The tiny creature scuttled across the room.

if you want the readers to dislike it.

Mistake!

That links to the second mistake you should avoid. If you are using interesting, varied and expressive verbs in your writing, you may not need lots of adverbs.

For example, you don't need to write:

He screamed shrilly when he found the scorpion in his room.

because a scream is always a shrill sound,

and you don't need to write:

The thief crept quietly into the jeweller's vault.

because all creeping is quiet; there is no such action as loud creeping.

Crossover

There is similar advice about overuse and unnecessary use in the information about **adjectives** on page 16.

Mistake!

The third mistake to avoid is mixing up the words 'well' and 'good'.

'Well' is an adverb. It tells us about how someone does something. It affects the verb:

She writes very well.   **I'm not feeling very well today.**

'Good' is an adjective. It tells us about a noun:

It's a really good book.   **I love a good long walk on Christmas Day.**

If someone asks you how you are today, I hope the answer would be:

I'm very well, thanks.

You would be saying that you feel fit and healthy. The adverb 'well' goes with the verb of being that we find in 'I'm' (I am). However, if you answered:

I'm good, thanks.

that would sound very arrogant. You would be saying that you are a good person, because the adjective 'good' goes with the pronoun 'I'. (You will learn about **pronouns** on page 35.)

Bringing it all together

▶ Verbs and adverbs

Now that you have learned about verbs, and the adverbs that often go with them, you are ready to revise your learning and check that you remember it.

❯ Verbs

You learned that some verbs are about actions or events – things that happen. Some verbs are about feelings. And, there is a very tricky irregular verb about **being**.

Read the passage. When you find a verb about an <u>action or event</u>, **underline** it. When you find a verb about a feeling, **draw a box** round it. When you find any part of the verb of being, **draw a bubble** round it. One of each has been marked for you as an example.

It <u>snowed</u> so hard that day that all the buses were cancelled. I was bored, because my boss had told everyone to stay at home until the snowstorm was over. I hated having nothing to do. I wanted to go and see a film, but the cinema was shut too. Then I thought I could make some cookies or bake a cake. (I love cake and I totally adore chocolate chip cookies.) I looked in the kitchen cupboard. There were no eggs. There was butter in the fridge. So I could make cookies but not cake. Then I realised I had no flour. I struggled through thick snow to the supermarket, but it was shut too. I stumbled home, grumbling under my breath the whole time, and made two slices of toast instead.

❯ Adverbs

You learned that some adverbs are about **how** a verb is done. Some adverbs are about **when** a verb is done, some are about **where** it is done and some are about **how much** it is done.

Read the passage. When you find an adverb that tells us <u>how</u> a verb is done, **underline** it. When you find an adverb about when or where a verb is done, **draw a box** round it. When you find an adverb that tells us about how much a verb is done, **draw a bubble** round it. One of each has been marked for you as an example.

I consumed the first slice of toast <u>greedily</u>, with the butter dripping warmly down my fingers. As soon as it was gone, I immediately turned to the second slice. It was nowhere to be seen. It had completely disappeared. I had had it just a few seconds earlier. Where could it be? Just then I heard a noise. Someone or something was eagerly destroying my other bit of toast, which was odd because I thought I was totally alone in the house.

▶ Pronouns

Read this passage, and decide what seems odd about it.

Yesterday, my family's pet cat Clara got stuck up a tree. Clara getting stuck up a tree all happened really quickly. Clara was lying on the family home's doorstep in the sun having a little nap when a dog went past. The dog wasn't a nasty dog. The dog was Biscuit. Biscuit lives just up the street and Biscuit comes past with Biscuit's owner June every day. Biscuit saw Clara and barked. Biscuit was only being friendly, but Clara got a fright and Clara woke up really suddenly. Clara yowled, and Biscuit thought Clara wanted to play a game, so Biscuit came running up the path towards my family's front door wagging Biscuit's tail and barking. Clara yowled even louder and jumped up the tree, scrambling up the tree's lowest branches until Clara got to the tree's very top. Once Clara was up there, Clara looked down and panicked about how high off the ground Clara was. That's how Clara got stuck. How the family got Clara back down is another story altogether.

Did the story get annoying? Did it feel repetitive? Were you bored?

The problem is that the story didn't have any **pronouns**. Without pronouns, the little paragraph just above this one would say:

> Did the story get annoying? Did the story feel repetitive? Were all the people reading and using this book bored?

A **pronoun** takes the place of a noun. Using pronouns saves us from having to repeat nouns in our writing. The main pronouns are:

I	it	him	he	they	us
you	we	her	she	me	them

The **possessive pronouns** – pronouns that show something belongs to, or goes along with, someone or something – are:

my/mine	his	its	their/theirs
your/yours	her/hers	our/ours	

Pronouns work incredibly hard for us: if they are used properly we hardly even notice them. Here's the story of the cat and the tree again, this time using pronouns.

Yesterday, our pet cat Clara got stuck up a tree. It all happened really quickly. She was lying on our doorstep in the sun having a little nap when a dog went past. It wasn't a nasty dog: it was Biscuit. He lives just up the street and comes past with his owner June every day. Biscuit saw Clara and barked. He was only being friendly, but she got a fright and woke up really suddenly. Clara yowled, and Biscuit thought she wanted to play a game, so he came running up the path towards our front door wagging his tail and barking. She yowled even louder and jumped up the tree, scrambling up its lowest branches until she got to its very top. Once she was up there, Clara looked down and panicked about how high off the ground she was. That's how she got stuck. How we got her back down is another story altogether.

Did you notice that we didn't replace every common or proper noun with a pronoun? Our writing always needs **some** nouns so that it makes sense. It's important to use some nouns to help us keep track of who is doing what and to make characters feel real.

 Building

Find the **pronouns** in these sentences.

1 A group of students got off the bus with their arms full of books.

2 I rubbed my tired eyes and tried to concentrate on my book, but it was really boring.

3 I asked him if he wanted to see the new superhero film, but he said he had seen it already.

4 The restaurant was crowded, but the manager was really helpful and she found them a table in the corner.

5 The nurse was obviously busy, but he kindly answered all our questions.

6 Granny knitted me a jumper. She's very kind, but I'm not wearing it: its sleeves go down to my knees and the wool is really itchy.

ᐧ|ᐨ|ᐧ Strengthening

Find the **pronouns** in these sentences. Say which common or proper noun each pronoun takes the place of. The first one has been done for you as an example.

1   The children went to pick brambles. They found lots of them on the path down by the river.

    they = children   them = brambles

2   The students wandered off towards the university. They were so busy talking that they paid no attention to anyone else around them.

3   The story was about an ancient wizard trying to teach a young boy. He kept turning him into different animals and putting him into dangerous situations.

4   Ben said the film was far too long and he spoiled it for me by telling me how it ended.

5   The food was delicious, but it was so expensive that I don't think we will ever go back there.

6   The nurse explained that my sister would have to stay in the hospital overnight. He said she had broken her arm so badly that she would need an operation the next day to put metal pins in it.

7   The jumper is bright pink too and has a unicorn on it. I don't think my gran has any idea how old I am or what I do: I just can't wear it to read the news on national TV.

Extending

Let's continue the story of Clara, the cat who got stuck up the tree. Re-write this passage, replacing the nouns with **pronouns** when you think it is appropriate to do so. Remember that you do not have to replace every single one – we need some common and proper nouns to help us keep track and to make the characters feel alive.

So there was Clara, stuck at the top of the tree and yowling Clara's head off. All the members of my family were standing at the bottom of the tree, trying to get Clara down by calling Clara's name. That didn't work. Then our family tried to entice Clara down by opening a tin of Clara's favourite cat food and waving the tin of Clara's favourite cat food in the air above our family's heads so that Clara would smell the delicious aroma and come down. That didn't work.

→

Our family was almost ready to phone the fire brigade when Biscuit, who had been sitting there the whole time, saved our family the trouble and embarrassment of admitting we had lost control of the family's cat. Biscuit wandered up the family's garden path and sat down on Clara's blanket in the patch of sunlight by the front door. Clara saw Biscuit. Clara was furious. That was Clara's blanket and Clara's patch of sunlight! How dare Biscuit try to take all of that away from Clara? Within seconds, Clara had scrambled back down the tree and sprinted up the family's garden path, hissing at Biscuit as Clara ran. Biscuit whimpered and gave up Biscuit's spot in the sun.

So far in our work on pronouns you have learned how these incredibly useful little words save us having to repeat much bigger and more noticeable common and proper nouns. It's time now to build up our knowledge and to learn about some more advanced uses of pronouns.

›› Reflexive pronouns

We use **reflexive pronouns** when the **subject** of a sentence – the person who does the verb – is the same as the **object** of the sentence – the person the verb gets done to. For example:

I hit **myself** in the face with my own umbrella. (The hitter got hit.)

He locked **himself** out of the house. (The person who locked the door was the person who got locked out.)

They defended **themselves** against the enemy. (The people who did the defending were the people who needed to be defended.)

Reflexive pronouns all end in -self or -selves:

myself	himself	itself	yourselves
yourself	herself	ourselves	themselves

 Crossover

You learned about **subjects** of verbs on page 18 and will learn more on page 40.

Use the list of **reflexive pronouns** in the box above to help you complete these sentences. You will need to use each reflexive pronoun once.

1 He could hear _____ shouting, but no one paid him any attention.

2 She had a very high opinion of _____, though I could never see what was so wonderful about her.

3 The hedgehog sensed danger coming and rolled _____ into a ball.

4 I spent the day all by _____, wandering along the beach collecting shells.

5 We helped _____ to pies, sausage rolls and sandwiches from the buffet table.

6 The faster the children ran down the hill, the more they tripped _____ up.

7 Please fill in the answers to these questions, and do be as honest as you can about _____.

8 If you could all please pick up pens, paper and clipboards for _____ from the table by the door, that will save us a lot of time later.

Mistake!

One important reason for knowing about reflexive pronouns is because people often overuse them or use them in the wrong way. People do this because they think these words sound **formal**, or fancy, so they think that using these words will make them sound more clever. They say things like:

> If you have any suggestions about how we could improve our team newsletter, please pass these to myself.

> This car would be perfect for yourself and your family.

Using a reflexive pronoun in this way is just wrong and being wrong can never make you sound clever.

Read the following sentences. Some of them use reflexive pronouns correctly. Some of them use reflexive pronouns incorrectly. Identify the right and wrong uses.

1 I haven't seen you for ages. How's yourself today?

2 If you can fetch your tickets yourself, I'll go and find out which platform the train will be leaving from.

3 I am happy to speak for myself; I don't need anyone else speaking for myself.

4 We all watched himself step out on stage, full of his own importance.

5 You have all worked very hard. Why don't you treat yourselves to an afternoon off or a night out?

6 This would be the ideal holiday for yourselves: the kids will love the beach club and the two of you will enjoy the evening entertainment in the hotel.

Now that you have learned how to avoid mistakes with reflexive pronouns, let's look at another pronoun mistake many speakers and writers make.

>> Using the pronouns I and me

When you write or speak about something that you and others do or did together, you should put the other people **first** and put yourself **afterwards**. To help you to remember this, tell yourself that it is always polite to put other people first. (Did you notice the reflexive pronoun in that sentence? Well done if you did!)

For example:

My friends and I go to the park.   My sister and I watched TV.

In the examples above, it is correct to use the word 'I' to write about yourself because the people are the subjects in each sentence. (Remember, the subject is the person in a sentence who does the verb. You learned that on page 18.)

Sometimes the people will be the object of the sentence. (Remember, the object is the person the verb is done to. You learned that on page 27.) In this case, you use the word 'me' to write about yourself, and you still, politely, put the other people first.

She gave presents to my brother and me.   The cake was for my dad and me.

So far, so good. You are still being polite and putting other people first. Sadly that's where some people start to make mistakes.

Mistake!

Some people think you always have to write '_____ and I' because that sounds formal or polite. They end up writing things like this:

That was a lovely experience for my mum and I.

Whenever she went abroad, my auntie sent a postcard to Gregor and I.

If you can't see why that's wrong, remove the other person from the sentence and read it again:

That was a lovely experience for I.

Whenever she went abroad, my auntie sent a postcard to I.

You should be able to hear how wrong that sounds. The writer should have used 'me' both times.

For each sentence, decide whether the missing word should be 'I' or 'me'. HINT! Try taking the other person out of the sentence and check if it still works:

1 My class and _____ got taken on a trip to the trampoline park.

2 The ref shouted at Finlay and _____.

3 Jamal and _____ caught a bus to the centre of town.

4 The pizza was for Ruben and _____ but the garlic bread was just for _____.

5 Two paramedics helped Phoebe and _____ when we got knocked off our bikes.

6 My boss and _____ met that afternoon to talk about the new project.

7 The scout asked Lucy and _____ to stay behind after the match.

8 The band played our favourite song for my wife and _____.

9 My new neighbour and _____ met each other on the stairs.

10 My grandad went out to his bowling club every Thursday while Granny and _____ stayed at home.

▶ Prepositions

Like the pronouns that you have just been learning about, **prepositions** are small but extremely useful and hard-working words.

> **Prepositions** show how one thing relates to another. Many prepositions are about space:
>
> The hawk hovered **above** the cornfield.
>
> or about time:
>
> I had heard of Rachel long **before** I actually met her.
>
> A preposition always comes before a **noun** or a **pronoun**.

There are lots of English prepositions. Here is a list of some of the most common ones. They have been organised in order from shortest to longest.

up	in	on	at	to	up
of	by	off	for	near	till
upon	under	until	below	along	among
since	after	above	round	about	around
beyond	during	except	behind	before	beside
across	within	between	without	against	towards
through	beneath	on top of	alongside	underneath	in spite of

You **do not** have to learn the list. But it would be good to learn to recognise the words on the list, so that when you see one of these words you will know that it is a preposition.

One way to help your brain to notice things is to write them down. The act of writing makes your hand and brain work together in a way that is more powerful than just reading and trying to remember. This memory trick becomes even more powerful if your brain has to do something else with the information as you write it down.

To help you to remember which English words are the prepositions, write out the list again, but sort it into alphabetical order as you do this.

Crossover

You can learn more about **alphabetical order** on page 131.

Group task

This will take a few minutes to organise. Get everybody in your group or class to find two different objects. You will need them for a show and tell.

When you are all ready, each person should show the class their two chosen objects and tell the class something about those objects by using a **preposition**. They may need to touch or move the objects as they do this. For example:

The hoodie is hanging **on** the peg.

Carry on around the class until everyone has spoken. If someone gets stuck and cannot use a preposition to show the relationship between two objects, they can put the teacher on the spot to think of an instant preposition connection instead.

Building

Find the **prepositions** in each sentence.

1 The woman with the huge pram apologised to the owner of the dog for running over its tail.

2 She was an expert on mammals, but she knew very little about birds.

3 I was proud of my success in the audition.

4 The runners hurtled round the track towards the finish line.

5 The ball went smashing through the kitchen window, bounced off the worktop, rolled along the floor and got wedged behind the fridge.

6 It was going to be a good day out: Mum had the route loaded on her phone, Dad had packed a picnic in the coolbag and the kids had each brought a friend with them.

Strengthening

Think of a suitable **preposition** to fill each gap.

1 His pet rat liked to hide _____ the bed.

2 I think the film starts _____ half past seven.

3 I was totally disgusted to find what looked like a dead wasp _____ the plate of salad.

4 A group of builders was standing _____ the road.

5 When she heard him coming into the room, she tucked his birthday present _____ the sofa.

6 She wrote the story _____ him.

7 I don't know how it got lost because I'm sure I put it _____ the table.

8 Zookeepers chased the escaped tiger _____ the car park, _____ two fields and _____ an industrial estate before they caught up _____ it.

Extending

For this task you will need a list of prepositions beside you, either the version on page 42, or the alphabetical version you wrote out for yourself if you did that task.

Look again at the sentences you wrote in the **strengthening** task on page 43. For each gap where you used a preposition, decide which other prepositions would also make sense to fill that gap. HINT! There could be several right answers for some of the gaps.

One interesting thing about prepositions is the way that they affect the verbs that they follow. To 'give up' and to 'give in' both mean the same thing – to stop trying or to surrender. But some prepositions affect their verbs in very different ways.

Look at these groups of **verbs** with **prepositions**, then choose what to do next.

1 put up   put down   put away

2 run up   run round   run through

3 stand against   stand for   stand with

Now choose what to do:

> For a **strengthening** level task, explain the different meanings of the three different verb + preposition phrases in each group.

> For a **building** level task, use each of those verb + preposition phrases in a sentence to create nine sentences altogether.

> For an **extending** level task, do both of the above tasks for each verb + preposition phrase.

 Group task

Can the members of your class or group think of any more examples of where different prepositions make the same basic verb mean something very different?

Bringing it all together

▶ Pronouns and prepositions

Now that you have learned about pronouns, and how they stand in for nouns and help us to avoid annoying repetition, you are ready to revise your learning and check what you remember.

Choose a suitable pronoun to complete each sentence.

1   When the sun came out, _____ melted the snow.

2   Sienna's dad was pleased with _____ because _____ had told the truth.

3   Theo yelled so hard when _____ team scored that _____ nearly lost _____ voice.

4   Whenever _____ go abroad on holiday, _____ must make sure _____ have _____ passport with _____.

5   _____ am sure _____ put the coffee cup down beside _____ chair, but when _____ got back, _____ had disappeared.

6   When Zoe patted the dog that had been left outside Tesco, _____ wagged _____ tail at _____ and licked _____ hand.

7   _____ new room at the university was only a small one, but it was _____. _____ wouldn't have to share it with anybody, and that made _____ really happy.

8   When the bull chased my friends and _____ across the field, _____ made it safely to the gate, but then _____ slipped and got _____ covered in mud.

You have also been learning about prepositions. Here is a story you have seen several times before. Read it again. Underline each preposition.

> The café was packed. A barista at the counter was energetically pulling the lever on a vast, shiny machine, skilfully turning out cup after cup of steaming coffee. A speedy waiter slipped quickly between the tables, delivering plates of cake and bowls of spicy-smelling soup. In the corner, by the window, sat a small woman, quietly tapping away at the keys of a shiny laptop. She ignored everything around her, until she was disturbed by a sudden bark. An unsupervised toddler had pulled a dog's ears. The woman smiled sympathetically at the dog, scowled at the child and went back to whatever she was thinking about.

▶ Conjunctions

English words that begin with the letters con- often suggest the idea of 'with'. In fact, the word '*con*' in Italian and Spanish means 'with'. This is because Italian, Spanish and English all have roots in the ancient language of Latin, in which 'con' means 'with'.

A junction is a place where two (or more) roads meet.

So if 'con' suggests 'with' and a 'junction' is a joining of two or more roads, what do you think words called conjunctions do? Work this out for yourself, or discuss it with your group or class before you look at the explanation below.

> A **conjunction** (sometimes called a **connective**) is a word that can be used to join chunks of language together. Conjunctions can be used to join **clauses** to make **sentences** and to join short sentences together to make longer and more **complex sentences**.

Like the pronouns and prepositions that you have met already, conjunctions are small but very useful, hard-working words.

Here is a list of some of the most common English conjunctions, ordered from shortest to longest.

as	or	so	if	yet	for
and	but	nor	now	till	when
since	while	after	until	though	unless
before	so that	even if	whereas	because	although
whenever	wherever	as long as	as soon as	even though	

You **do not** have to learn the list. But it would be good to learn to recognise these words, so that when you see them or use them, you know they are conjunctions.

We are going to use the same memory-training trick that we did with the prepositions on page 42.

To help you to remember which English words are the conjunctions, write out the list again but sort it into alphabetical order as you do this. You can learn more about alphabetical order on page 131.

Building

Read this passage and find the **conjunctions**.

I was supposed to be doing a half-marathon on Sunday, but I could not take part in the race because I had hurt my foot. Although I could not run, I decided to go and watch anyway, since some of my friends from the running club were taking part.

So that I could get there without hurting my injured foot, I caught a bus near my flat. As it was the weekend, the bus got there very quickly, even though it had to go through the centre of town, and I soon reached the park where the finish line had been set up.

As soon as I got there I realised my mistake. While I like being outdoors, there wasn't much to do in the park except wait for the runners to arrive. Though my friends would have each other for company, and the run to keep them busy, I was alone and early and would be very bored very soon.

Yet there was something I could do to keep myself amused. I had my phone with me. Before I'd left home I'd downloaded the audiobook of my favourite crime writer's latest novel. There was a little wooden cabin nearby selling tea and cakes. As long as there was an empty table for me I'd be fine, and unless the staff got fed up with me, even if my friends were the last ones to cross the line, I could sit and listen happily for ages.

Strengthening

In this task, you are given two sentences each time. Choose a **conjunction** from the list below and put it in the middle to join the two shorter, simpler sentences into one longer one. The first one has been done for you as an example.

We'll start with some of the simplest, most frequently used conjunctions:

➤ and ➤ so ➤ but ➤ because

1 I like broccoli. I detest Brussels sprouts.

I like broccoli, but I detest Brussels sprouts.

2 The howling wind was bringing slates down off the roof. We stayed indoors.

3 Her dad offered to pay her £10. She washed the car and hoovered the inside.

4 We knew we might be too late for the film. We headed out anyway.

5 Alice is on the football team. She is in the swimming squad.

6 The yoga class was cancelled. The tutor was on holiday.

7 She booked a holiday that afternoon. She paid for her new glasses too.

Let's add some more conjunctions to the list. Each time use a **conjunction** to join two shorter, simpler sentences into one longer one.

- because
- though
- when
- where

- as
- after
- until
- but

- and
- so
- or
- before

- while
- although

1   She always revised thoroughly. She sat exams.

2   He had baked an utterly delicious, beautifully decorated cake. He knew the judges would love it.

3   Grandad could go to the woodwork class on Thursday. He could play in the darts match.

4   He tried politely to keep the conversation going. He was bored and didn't like talking about football.

5   I listen to podcasts on my phone. I try to walk my 10,000 steps for the day.

6   The box did not sink at once. It was full of metal.

7   The float parade meandered past. The children cheered and waved.

8   The game ended. The referee blew the whistle.

9   The ships remained in the harbour. The weather improved.

10 The cyclist was hurtling down hill in the rain. He slipped and crashed into a wall.

11 I grew up in a quiet village. I prefer city life.

12 I was sure I'd seen someone breaking in to the house. I phoned the police.

13 She had no idea what they were talking about. She hadn't seen that TV programme last night.

14 The detectives returned to the patch of waste ground. Witnesses said they had seen some suspicious characters late last night.

15 He was sick. He ate two pizzas and a litre of ice cream all by himself.

16 I have three female cousins. I have two male ones.

So far you have used conjunctions **between** two sentences to join them up into one longer and more complex sentence. However, you can also use a conjunction **at the start** of your new, longer sentence. You can also join more than two sentences together this way. Look at these sentences:

The traffic warden passed the car. She looked carefully at it. She took a picture of it with her phone.

By using 'as' at the beginning and 'and' later, we can join up these three sentences:

> As the traffic warden passed the car, she looked carefully at it and took a picture of it with her phone.

 Extending

Join up each of the groups of sentences to make one, more complex, **sentence**. Start each one with the **bold** word in the brackets. HINT! Look at the example above to see how you can miss out other small or repeated words.

1   My friend left late that evening. I locked the door. I went to bed. **(when)**

2   The taxi stopped. The door opened. A man stepped out. **(when)**

3   They raced through the forest. She tripped over a sprawling tree root. She landed awkwardly. **(as)**

4   We rowed away from the shore. We heard a shout. We saw a young woman rushing to the water's edge. **(as)**

5   My grandparents came through the arrivals gate. I dropped my bag and coat on the floor. I rushed up to hug them. **(when)**

6   It began to snow. I decided to stay in all day. I turned the central heating up. **(because)**

7   It had started snowing. I put on my warmest jacket. I went out. **(although)**

8   The chicken was roasting in the oven. I made a pot of soup. I made some pasta sauce. **(while)**

Different conjunctions can do very different things to the meaning of a sentence. A sentence that begins:

> I will go to the beach if ...

will be very different from one that begins:

> I will go to the beach unless ...

Here are three sentence openings:	Here are seven conjunctions:		
I will visit the moon in my lifetime ...	if	when	unless	and
She will become a doctor ...			
Forecasters say there will be floods this weekend ...	although	while	because

Now choose what to do:

➤ For a **building** level task, pick **one** sentence opening. Use **at least four** of the seven conjunctions to make **four** very different sentences from the same opening.

➤ For a **strengthening** level task, pick **one** sentence opening. Use **all seven** of the conjunctions to make **seven** very different sentences from the same opening.

➤ For an **extending** level task, use **all three** sentence openings. Use **at least four** of the seven conjunctions each time to make **four** very different sentences from each opening.

➤ If you are feeling super-confident, use **all three** sentence openings. Use **all seven** conjunctions each time to make **seven** very different sentences from each opening. You will end up with 21 sentences.

 Crossover

When you reach page 119, in the chapter about sentences and paragraphs, you will learn about **main clauses**. You have just practised joining chunks of language together with conjunctions to make longer, more sophisticated sentences. Each of those language chunks is a main clause.

You have now met seven English parts of speech. You know about nouns and the adjectives that describe them. You have met verbs and the adverbs that tell us about them. You have met the very useful, short pronouns that save us repeating nouns and the prepositions that tell us how nouns and pronouns relate to each other. You have used conjunctions to connect sentences together more fluently.

There are just two more parts of speech, two more word types, for you to meet.

▶ Articles

Like pronouns and prepositions, articles are tiny words that work incredibly hard, yet you probably don't even notice them.

> Articles point us towards the nouns in a sentence. In English, the articles are:
>
> a   an   the

We call 'a' or 'an' the indefinite article, because it helps to point us towards something quite general. The sentence:

I'd love a puppy.

tells us someone wants a canine pet. They are not particularly fussy, or may not be very sure yet, about what sort of dog, or which puppy, they want.

We use 'a' before words that start with a consonant sound. We use 'an' before words that begin with a vowel sound, to make these words easer to say.

> **An** eagle is a huge bird, but **a** robin is much, much smaller.

 Crossover

You will learn more about **vowels** and **consonants** on page 133.

We call 'the' the **definite article**, because it helps to point us towards a definite, certain, particular thing.

> I'd love to have the puppy with the wonky ear and the black patch over its eye.

We usually use the definite article 'the' in situations where it is clear what we are referring to. If you use a phrase like 'the man' or 'the car', your readers should never be wondering, 'What man?' or 'Which car?'

Read the following passage. For each numbered gap, decide if you should use 'a' or 'an' or 'the'. HINT! When you are deciding between 'a' or 'an', remember to think about how the words sound, not how they are spelled or how they look on the page.

I wanted something to eat, but what? I looked in **(1)** _____ fridge. There was **(2)** _____ small amount of bacon, and **(3)** _____ egg, but **(4)** _____ bottle of ketchup was empty, apart from **(5)** _____ thin, solid layer right at **(6)** _____ bottom. Any fry-up made of that sad collection was not going to fill me up.

Maybe I could make **(7)** _____ egg into something else. I searched **(8)** _____ rest of **(9)** _____ kitchen. I found some sugar in **(10)** _____ bag in **(11)** _____ cupboard under **(12)** _____ stove, and there was some flour in another bag in **(13)** _____ same cupboard. Then I spotted **(14)** _____ lemon in **(15)** _____ fruit bowl. That gave me **(16)** _____ idea.

I went back to **(17)** _____ fridge and made **(18)** _____ exciting find. Milk! Lots of milk! I could easily whip up some pancakes.

Bringing it all together

▶ Conjunctions and articles

❭ Conjunctions

You have learned about conjunctions and about how they can be used to join short sentences to create longer, more interesting ones. You are ready to revise your learning and check what you remember.

Here is a reminder of some of the conjunctions you have been using:

- after
- if
- unless
- wherever

- although
- before
- until
- whether

- as
- since
- whenever
- which

- because

Choose a suitable conjunction from the list above to fit each gap in the story.

(1) _____ we go camping, and (2) _____ we go, we always take lots of kit with us. (3) _____ Claire loves to cook on a campfire, we take lots of burgers, (4) _____ Hamish is vegan and needs to have the ones made out of soya mince.

(5) _____ I am quite a cautious person, we take all sorts of waterproofs and wet weather gear, (6) _____ the forecast is for blazing sunshine. (7) _____ it might be cold at night, I bring the thickest sleeping bags. (8) _____ we head off, I also insist on checking that we have packed everything properly.

(9) _____ Samir loves hillwalking, we take a bundle of maps, (10) _____ he sits looking at each night by the campfire (11) _____ he plans the next day's expedition. (12) _____ we have phoned home to tell someone our plan for the day, he won't let us head off on our hike: he says it's much safer that way.

(13) _____ it all goes to plan or not, we always enjoy our trips. (14) _____ I get home, I realise how good it has been for me to get away from city life.

Bringing it all together

❯ Articles

You have also been learning about articles. Decide whether each of these nouns or noun phrases would come after 'a' or 'an'. HINT! Remember to think about how the words sound, not how they are spelled or how they look on the page.

- ➤ envelope
- ➤ book
- ➤ caravan
- ➤ towering building
- ➤ knee
- ➤ knot
- ➤ unicorn
- ➤ FBI investigator
- ➤ drip
- ➤ app
- ➤ hourly rate
- ➤ elegant dress
- ➤ wrinkle
- ➤ bed
- ➤ honesty box
- ➤ curious puzzle

▶ Interjections

Interjections are words that express a short burst of emotion, such as a warning or something that is shouted out. They are usually used on their own – which means that they need a capital letter – and are followed by an **exclamation mark**:

Hey!	Hooray!	Eek!	Ouch!	D'oh!
Phew!	Wow!	Yuk!	Rubbish!	Oh!

Some interjections show hesitation or a pause. They don't usually have an exclamation mark, but they might be followed by an **ellipsis** – three dots that show the sentence tailing off.

Um ... Er ...

 Crossover

You will learn much more about exclamation marks on page 60.

Look at the ten interjections that come with exclamation marks in the explanation box above. For each one, give a reason or a situation where that interjection could be the perfect word to use.

For example, if you saw somebody who was so busy looking at their phone that they did not know they were about to walk into some tables outside a café, you might shout, 'Hey!' at them.

2 Punctuation

In the introduction to this book you saw some examples of how grammar affects meaning. (You can look back to page vi if you want to see them again.) Most of those examples were about punctuation – the little tiny marks, lines and dots that we use to shape and structure our sentences. Punctuation marks don't really mean anything by themselves, but they powerfully organise words to create meanings. As the examples on page vii showed, we can keep all the same words in the same order but make huge differences to meaning by changing the punctuation marks that sit around and between those words.

▶ Full stops, question marks and exclamation marks

We're going to start with three of the most common punctuation marks. Each of these marks can be found at the end of a sentence.

> Most English sentences end with a **full stop**. It looks like a dot and sits on the line:
>
> I like dogs.

> If a sentence asks a **question**, it ends with a **question mark**:
>
> Do you like dogs?

> We use an **exclamation mark** at the end of a sentence to show a strong emotion like anger or surprise or to show that the speaker is shouting:
>
> Stop that dog!

≫ Full stops

Most English sentences end with a **full stop**. Unless there is a really good reason for using one of the other sentence endings, a sentence should end with a full stop.

Crossover

Every sentence you write should also start with a capital letter. You can learn more about using **capital letters** on pages 4 and 112.

 Building

Write out each group of words, dividing it into **sentences** as you go by working out where to put **full stops** and **capital letters**. The text in brackets at the end of each group will tell you how many sentences to make.

1. the storm began slowly a wind blew in from the west (**2 sentences**)

2. clouds gathered the temperature dropped (**2 sentences**)

3. trees bent back and forwards in the wind it got colder and colder (**2 sentences**)

4. the temperature was now below freezing sheep out in the fields huddled together for warmth the first snowflakes fell (**3 sentences**)

5. at first the snow seemed harmless it drifted gently down and filled the potholes in city streets drivers turned on their headlights (**3 sentences**)

6. the snow grew thicker it was a true blizzard now nobody could see more than a few metres in front of themselves (**3 sentences**)

7. conditions on the roads became more challenging cars slithered and skidded if drivers slammed on their brakes this only made things worse the BBC broadcast a weather warning (**4 sentences**)

8. shops shut early all the schools were closed and the pupils were sent home people were told not to travel unless their journey was essential lots of people were secretly quite pleased that they wouldn't have to go to work the next day (**4 sentences**)

Strengthening

Write out each group of words, dividing it into **sentences** as you go by working out where to put **full stops** and **capital letters**. This time you will have to work out for yourself how many sentences there are in each group.

1. dinosaurs first appeared on our planet a very long time ago they were enormous

2. people have always found dinosaurs fascinating perhaps this is because we know a lot about them but no human has ever seen one

3   there have been many films that have put people and dinosaurs in scenes together some of those films are set in prehistoric times some of them are set in modern theme parks they are all totally untrue

4   dinosaurs lived here a very long time ago they also lived for a long time humans appeared more recently we have actually not been here very long compared to dinosaurs

5   we have known about dinosaurs for 200 years scientists keep learning new things about them and discovering the fossils of unknown species we now know that some dinosaurs had feathers like birds others came in vibrant shades of blue and green

 Extending

Write **three** sentences about what has happened to you, or what you have done, **today**. Check that each one starts with a **capital letter** and ends with a **full stop**.

Write **three** sentences about what has happened to you, or what you have done, **this week or this month**. Check that each one starts with a **capital letter** and ends with a **full stop**.

>> Question marks

If a sentence asks a question, it ends with a question mark.

 Building

Match the questions with the answers to complete the riddles.

1 How do you know the sea likes you?	**A** water
2 What has a cap, but no head to wear it on?	**B** a coin
3 What did the road say to the bridge?	**C** heat because you can catch cold
4 What cannot walk but runs?	**D** because of the waves
5 What has a head and tail with no body in between?	**E** envelope
6 Where do aliens put their teaspoons?	**F** You make me cross.
7 What moves faster, heat or cold?	**G** a cold
8 Which fish can mend a piano?	**H** a bottle
9 Which eight-letter word has just one letter in it?	**I** a tuna fish
10 What can you catch but never throw?	**J** in their flying saucers

Strengthening

Read these sentences. Decide whether each one should end with a **full stop** or with a **question mark**.

1   When does the school break up for the holidays

2   I wonder how the magician did that trick

3   Where is that hammer I left in the toolbox

4   How well can Rajid swim

5   Tell me if I have this wrong

6   I want to know who wrote this text message

7   Would you please all make less noise

8   Tell me why you asked that question

 Extending

Pick **one** of these characters. Write **five questions** that person might ask. Make sure each question starts with a **capital letter** and ends with a **question mark**.

A doctor speaking to a patient who has a very sore arm

A journalist talking to the Prime Minister

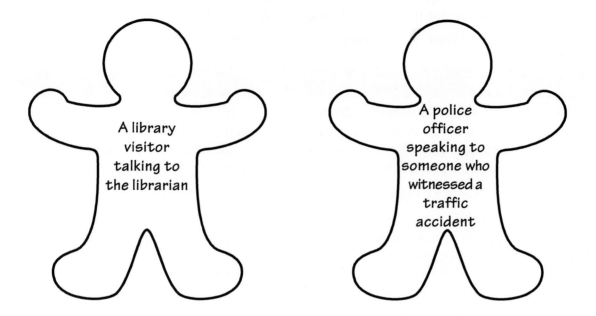

A library visitor talking to the librarian

A police officer speaking to someone who witnessed a traffic accident

If you want to give yourself a challenge, pick another character and do the task again.

 Group task

Start by working alone. Here are five prompt words:

➤ invisible ➤ film ➤ holiday ➤ magic ➤ achievement

Make up an interesting question for each of the five prompt words. For example, if you had the prompt word 'animal' you might ask, 'What is your favourite animal?' or 'Which animal are you most afraid of?'

Write down your questions, making sure you use **capital letters** and **question marks**.

Now find a partner. Ask them the questions. You may want to make a note of the answers you hear.

Once everyone has had a chance to ask, and to answer, five questions, feed back to the class. Tell your classmates:

➤ the most interesting question that you were asked

➤ the most interesting answer that your partner told you.

Questions often, but not always, begin with one of these key words:

➤ Why   ➤ What   ➤ When   ➤ Where   ➤ How

 Group task

Take a few seconds to look around the room you are in. Everyone in your group or class should then take it in turns to make up a question based on something you can see from where you are sitting. The questions should all start with one of the five key starter words above. For example, you might ask:

Why is the classroom clock stuck at half past two?

If your teacher thinks that the same starter word has been used too often, or notices that some of the starter words are not being used, they might tell you which starter word to use.

>> Exclamation marks

We use an exclamation mark at the end of a sentence to show a strong emotion like anger or surprise, or to show that the speaker is shouting.

 Crossover

Exclamation marks go with the interjections you can learn about on page 54.

Mistake!

The biggest mistake that people make with exclamation marks is using too many of them. If you overuse exclamation marks it will feel like you are always shouting, which gets very tiring for the reader. The writer of this book used to have a boss who sent emails with titles like:

Monday morning tasks!!!!!!!!

which made it feel as if her boss, her computer and her emails were all screaming at her. It is **always totally wrong** to use more than one exclamation mark at a time. It is often wrong, or at least not necessary, to use any at all.

Think of exclamation marks as being like unicorns – amazing and powerful because they are so rare and unusual.

 Building

Use **three full stops, two question marks** and **one exclamation mark** to complete this message:

> How are you What is the weather like where you are I bet it's warmer than here It's freezing here Ugh You were so right to move

 Strengthening

There are **six** places in this story where it would be all right to use an **exclamation mark**. Work out where they would go.

> The day trip started badly. We were cruising along the bypass at 60 miles an hour when we suddenly saw a sign that said:
>
> SLOW DOWN WORKMEN IN ROAD
>
> I did as I was told and slowed down. By this time the children were arguing in the back seat. 'Stop' I snapped.

They kept squabbling.

'Now' I yelled.

They fell quiet at last, and we drove on towards the safari park. I knew they'd like it when we got there: they were desperate to see the meerkat colony.

As we passed through the massive gate in the woven metal fence, another sign warned us:

LIONS STAY IN YOUR CAR

Sure enough, a pride of lions was lounging on the grass ahead of us, lazily flicking their tails in the sun.

'Wow' said my daughter, who has always been a bit bloodthirsty.

'Help' said my son, who has a rather overactive imagination, and was probably picturing us all becoming Simba snacks.

Bringing it all together

▶ Full stops, question marks and exclamation marks

Write out each group of words, dividing it into sentences by using full stops and capital letters.

1   i was walking past the patch of waste ground when I heard a noise it sounded like an animal struggling **(2 sentences)**

2   it wasn't a bird it wasn't a cat either from the way the bushes rustled as it moved around I was sure it was something bigger **(3 sentences)**

3   i'm quite cautious but I love animals it would be awful if one was trapped or in pain **(2 sentences)**

4   feeling pretty brave, I pushed my way through a gap in the rusty fence the ground inside was muddy and hard to walk on I had to shove my way through lots of vegetation too it seemed like no one had been there for years **(4 sentences)**

Write out each group of words, dividing it into sentences by using full stops and capital letters. Work out for how many sentences there are in each group.

5   the sound of movement grew louder something was struggling and crying maybe it had got caught up in all that undergrowth

6   as I got closer I could see a shape moving the creature had a black and white snout it was a badger

7   badgers are strong I couldn't understand why it was stuck then I realised what was happening

8   it was an adult badger and it wasn't stuck at all it was trying to save one of its cubs the little creature's paw had got tangled up in some dumped rubbish the parent was trying to untangle it

9   i wanted to help but I knew badgers could be fierce they have a powerful bite and I did not want to get bitten I stayed well back as quietly as I could I pulled out my phone and called the RSPCA

10 a rescue team soon arrived they fired a tranquilliser at the adult badger from a safe distance and sent it to sleep then they were able to go in and free the cub

Use capital letters, **four** full stops, **two** question marks and **one** exclamation mark to complete this passage.

> did you get my message I sent it days ago I still haven't had an answer I need to know what you would like to do on your birthday what do you want as a present for goodness sake I can't organise anything if you won't answer me

▶ Apostrophes

You have now learned about three of the most common punctuation marks: the full stop, question mark and exclamation mark. They are all used at the end of sentences.

We will move on now to an important mark that some people find a little confusing.

> An **apostrophe** is a small punctuation mark that hovers just above written or printed words. You can see it in the examples below.
>
> It is used for **contraction**, to show that letters and spaces have been missed out when words are combined to make a shorter word:
>
> > don't   hasn't   can't   didn't
>
> It is also used for **ownership**, to show possession or a strong connection:
>
> > our dog's bed   the students' exam papers   the children's room

❯❯ The contraction apostrophe

You can use an **apostrophe** to show that letters, and spaces between words, have been missed out to make words shorter and therefore easier to say. The apostrophe goes into the place where the letters and spaces have been removed. For example:

> that is = that's   we are = we're

 Building

Look at these **contractions**. Write them out in full. The first one has been done for you as an example.

1 they'll
   they will

2 I'd

3 haven't

4 I'm

5 don't

6 won't

7 let's

⊪⎮⊪ Strengthening

Write out these phrases in their **contracted** form, using **apostrophes** where you need them to show that letters and spaces have been missed out.

- ➤ they would
- ➤ I have
- ➤ we will
- ➤ I am not
- ➤ you would not have

- ➤ he did not
- ➤ you are
- ➤ it is
- ➤ we might have
- ➤ I had not

- ➤ here is
- ➤ she cannot
- ➤ they are
- ➤ we were not
- ➤ he is

Extending

Write out this story using **apostrophes** in the right places to **contract** some of the words.

> Nadia had a secret. She had taken her dad's recipe book. Nadia's dad was on a diet and she thought it would be a good idea if he could not make any more of his famous creamy curries.
>
> First she thought she would hide the book in the laundry basket, but he would find it when it was his turn to fill the washing machine.
>
> Then she considered her little brother's bedroom, but there was a note on the door that said, 'If you come in here, I will shoot you with my space blaster.'
>
> She wondered about putting the book in the cat's basket, but she knew it would hate to sleep on something lumpy.
>
> Finally, she put the book in the cupboard with the curry spices. After all, her dad was not meant to be looking in there.

Mistake!

Some people mix up words that use a contraction apostrophe with other words that sound or look similar but have a different meaning. Be very careful with these contractions:

you're is short for 'you are'	You're very tall.
your means belonging to you	Give me your plate.
we're is short for 'we are'	We're going out now.
were is a verb	We were out all day yesterday.
they're is short for 'they are'	They're very noisy.
there tells us about a place	Put it over there.

The next exercise will let you practise using the tricky words explained on the previous page. Write out the paragraph, choosing the right word each time. The first letter of the word is there in **bold** to help you each time. HINT! Not every answer will be a word that uses a contraction apostrophe.

> I know **(1) y** going to New York on holiday. Have you got **(2) y** tickets yet? **(3) W** going to Barcelona. We **(4) w** going to go to Paris but **(5) t** having a big strike **(6) t** in the summer and we **(7) w** afraid we wouldn't be able to get home again if the airport **(8) t** got shut down. **(9) W** really looking forward to Barcelona but I'm sure **(10) y** going to have a great time in New York too. Will you show me **(11) y** photos when **(12) y** back home again?

Mistake!

Another mistake that some people make is not a mistake with contraction apostrophes but something that happens **because of how we hear** some words that use these apostrophes. Look at this example and especially at the three words in **bold**:

> I **should've** gone with her. I **could've** gone: I had lots of spare time that day. I **would've** been able to help her.

Because you understand this way of using apostrophes, you know that those three words could also be written out like this:

> I **should have** gone with her. I **could have** gone: I had lots of spare time that day. I **would have** been able to help her.

Sometimes we see people writing things like:

> I should **of** gone.   I would **of** helped.

The word 'of' in these sentences is wrong. People write it because they hear the **'ve' sound** in words like should've, could've and would've, but they think they are hearing an **'of' sound**. It's wrong to use 'of' when you write something like this, because there is no verb 'to of'. The verb is 'to have', and the -ve in those contractions is part of the word 'have'.

There is one more thing that you should know about the contraction apostrophe. Using apostrophes like this is considered to be not very formal. Contraction apostrophes are not incorrect English, but there are some **situations** where it would be thought wrong to use them. For example, if you are writing a job application, a formal business letter, a formal report or an essay, you should use the longer, more separate and more complete forms of words, rather than shortening them and pulling them together with the contraction apostrophe.

›› The ownership apostrophe

You have already learned how to use an apostrophe for contraction: to show that letters and spaces have been missed out. The second reason for using an apostrophe is to show ownership or, perhaps, a strong connection. For example:

our dog's bed   the students' exam papers   the children's room

This use of the apostrophe gets a little complicated, so we will build up your knowledge step by step.

› Step 1: using an ownership apostrophe when there is one, singular owner

If there is one 'owner', we show ownership by adding a letter -s to the end of the owner and putting an apostrophe before the -s. For example:

a house that belongs to her auntie = her auntie's house

the birthday of my friend = my friend's birthday

As you can see in these examples, using the ownership apostrophe allows us to write much shorter and more fluent phrases. They feel more natural to say and to write.

 Building

Turn each of these into a shorter, more natural phrase by using the **ownership apostrophe**.

1   a book that belongs to my sister
2   the tyre on a bus
3   the partner of a man
4   the door of a garden shed
5   the broken leg of a person called Ingrid
6   a hoodie belonging to a person called Diarmid
7   a teddy bear that belongs to a toddler
8   the pet snake that belongs to my neighbour
9   clothes for a baby
10 the tail of a monkey

Strengthening

Re-write this passage using the **ownership apostrophe** to create shorter and more natural phrases. To help you, the phrases that you need to change have been marked off with brackets.

> It was opening night. The (seats in the theatre) were all full. The (excitement of the audience) was obvious. So was the (nervousness of the star). She was pacing up and down backstage, reciting her first few lines to herself. Suddenly, she heard the (voice of the stage manager) warning her. Five minutes! (The pounding of her heart) grew even faster.

 Extending

Re-write this passage using the **ownership apostrophe** to create shorter and more natural phrases. This time it is up to you to work out where to make changes. **HINT!** You are looking for **six** examples to change.

> Suddenly she felt the hand of her co-star on her arm. The eyes of the man showed absolute terror.
>
> 'What on earth is wrong, Kyle?' she asked.
>
> 'I'm locked out of my dressing room!' he said.
>
> 'Don't panic. Get the key from the caretaker,' she suggested.
>
> 'He'll tell me off,' muttered Kyle. 'I am tired of all the moaning from that man.'
>
> She looked at her watch. Four minutes. Just enough time. She could nip into the office of the caretaker, grab the keys and be back in time for the start. 'I'll get what you need,' she said. 'Albert owes me a favour.'
>
> 'Why?'
>
> 'Because I organised all the free tickets for the primary school class his daughter is in when we did the panto last Christmas.'

❯ Step 2: using an ownership apostrophe when there is more than one owner

If there is more one 'owner', and if the plural ends with an -s, we show ownership by putting an apostrophe following the -s after the end of the owners. There is no need to add another -s after the apostrophe. For example:

> a football team for girls = the girls' football team

> a nest where several birds live = the birds' nest

> a car park for customers = the customers' car park

As before, using the ownership apostrophe allows us to write shorter, more natural phrases.

 Building

Turn each of these into a shorter, more natural phrase by using the **ownership apostrophe**.

1   a convention for film fans

2   the boss of some clowns

3   the noise from a number of phones

4   the branches of lots of trees

5   paint brushes belonging to lots of artists

6   pills being given to several patients

7   houses belonging to both of my grandmas

8   the birthdays of three of my friends

9   the quacks made by many ducks

10   the lids of some boxes

╶╢─╟╴ Strengthening

Re-write the passage on the next page using the **ownership apostrophe** to create shorter and more natural phrases. To help you, the phrases that you need to change have been marked off with brackets.

It was time for the annual spring clean at the zoo. The (pool for the penguins) was drained and scrubbed clean. While they were out of the water, the vet checked the (beaks and the feet of the penguins) to make sure they were clean and free from infection.

Over at the savannah park, the elephants were having a bath. The (buckets that belonged to the keepers) were filled with warm soapy water. The keepers sponged the (trunks of the elephants).

In the tropical rainforest, volunteers were gently cleaning the (shells of the turtles) and trimming the (claws of the iguanas).

 Extending

Re-write this passage using the **ownership apostrophe** to create shorter and more natural phrases. This time it is up to you to work out where to make changes. HINT! You are looking for **six** examples to change.

Meanwhile, there was lots of activity at the enclosure where the monkeys lived. The ropes on their climbing frames were checked and the doors of their huts were sanded down to take away any sharp splinters.

In the petting zoo, the cages for the rabbits were filled with soft fluffy bedding and the hutches for the guinea pigs were carefully cleaned out.

There was just one problem. The big cat expert was off with flu. No one else was qualified to go into the den for the lions.

> # Step 3: using an ownership apostrophe when there is more than one owner and the plural has an irregular spelling

 Crossover

On page 24 you learned that some verbs are **irregular** when they go into the **past tense**. They don't follow the simple basic rule of adding -ed to make a past tense. For example, the past tense of the regular verb 'to shout' is 'shouted', but the past tense of the irregular verb 'to go' is 'went'.

Some **nouns** are **irregular** when they go from **singular** to plural. Regular nouns add a letter -s at the end to make a plural. For example, 'dog' is a regular noun; its plural is 'dogs' with an -s at the end.

Irregular nouns make their plurals in many different ways. For example, 'child' is an irregular noun. The plural of 'child' is not 'childs' with an -s; it is 'children'.

When a noun has an irregular plural, this affects the way ownership apostrophes are used.

If there is more than one 'owner' and the irregular plural does not end with -s, we show ownership by adding an -s and putting an apostrophe before that -s:

> toilets for women = women's toilets

> winter coats for children = children's winter coats

Once again, using the ownership apostrophe allows us to write shorter, more natural phrases.

 Building

Turn each of these into a shorter, more natural phrase by using the **ownership apostrophe**.

1 the opinions of the people

2 food for the mice

3 the prickly spines of cacti

4 the wriggling of some lice

5 the voices of men

6 the union rep for the women

There is a **Bringing it all together** revision task on the next page. Once you have done it, and your knowledge of apostrophes is really strong, there is a little more to learn after that about the mistakes some apostrophe users make.

Bringing it all together

▶ Apostrophes

〉 The contraction apostrophe

Re-write the passage. When you see words in brackets, use the contraction apostrophe to shorten them. When you see an asterisk (*), decide if you need to replace it with **its** (which means belonging to it) or **it's** (which is short for 'it is' or 'it has').

> (We have) got to buy a new car. The one (we have) got now is worn out.
> * exhaust is falling off and * been making a terrible noise for weeks. (I am)
> sure we could take the car to the garage and ask them to fix that but that
> (will not) sort out * other problems. * tyres are badly worn and * left wing
> mirror is hanging off. (I am) sure * going to fall off and land in the road
> one day if we (do not) do something soon. Anyway, (I have) never liked
> the colour of * paintwork. Why (can we not) just buy a new car?

〉 The ownership apostrophe

Look at these phrases:

> the pupils reports   the teachers lessons

Write them out, using apostrophes, to show:

1   one pupil with several reports

2   lots of pupils who each get a report

3   lots of teachers who each taught many lessons

4   one teacher who taught some lessons

Re-write the passage, with ownership apostrophes in the right places, thinking carefully about singular and plural. All the clues you need are there to help you.

> The teams captain was feeling confident. She knew she was one of the
> best leaders they had ever had. Yes, all of the teams captains had been
> good, over many years, but she was the best.
>
> It wasn't quite like that when match day came. The players lined up, face
> to face. The teams captains were eyeball to eyeball. The linesmens flags
> were poised and ready. The ref lifted the whistle to her lips. The captains
> heart fluttered.

>> Apostrophe mistakes you can avoid

I said on page 64 that some people find apostrophes a little confusing. Not you, of course. Let's have a quick reminder of all the things you know and have practised about apostrophes.

You know that the **contraction apostrophe** shows where letters, and spaces between words, have been missed out. For example, 'that is' becomes 'that's'.

You know how to use the **ownership apostrophe** and how this changes:

➤ If the 'owner' is **singular**, the apostrophe goes before the -s. For example: 'My best friend's birthday is next week.'

➤ If the 'owners' are **plural**, you show this by putting the apostrophe at the end of the word, after the -s. For example: 'My friends' birthdays all seem to be in September.'

➤ If the **plural** is **irregular** and doesn't end in an -s, like men, women or children, you add an -s and put the apostrophe before it. For example: 'Have you seen the children's toys?'

Now that you know all of this, we can have a look at some of the mistakes that less confident writers make with apostrophes.

Mistake!

Some people wrongly use apostrophes in the possessive pronouns:

   his   its   yours   hers   ours   theirs

We can see how this might happen.

Those words are about ownership, and we already know that apostrophes have got something to do with ownership. But you can **only** use the ownership apostrophe with names and nouns, **never** with possessive pronouns.

 Crossover

You learned about possessive pronouns on page 36.

Mistake!

Some people wrongly use apostrophes in abbreviations like:

   MPs   CDs   DVDs

Again, we can see how this might happen. Those are short forms, and we already know that apostrophes have got something to do with shortening and contracting. But where would the apostrophes go? MP is short for 'Member of Parliament'. DVD is short for 'digital versatile disc'. Are you going to write M'P's or D'V'D's? Of course not. **Abbreviations** like those don't need apostrophes.

There's no need for this. There are no missing letters and nothing is being shortened. There is no reason at all to even think about using an apostrophe.

> # Mistake!
> Some people wrongly use apostrophes in dates like:
>
> 1890s   1940s   2030s

> # Mistake!
> Even worse, some people use apostrophes in plural nouns. Worst of all, some people put them in verbs. This is sometimes called the 'greengrocer's apostrophe', because we sometimes see it in shop windows, or the 'apostrofly', because these little marks have landed like unwelcome nasty little insects.

Look at these two signs. They contain lots of unnecessary apostrophes. Can you re-write them correctly?

1920's NIGHT

Friday 27th February
COCKTAIL'S
DANCING
DVD's of CLASSIC SILENT FILM'S

All under 18's
to be accompanied
by an adult.

Students's
meal deal.

✳ Sandwich + drink +
   crisp's + cookie £4.

✳ 10p donation from every
   deal sold on Friday's goe's
   to St John's hospital.

▶ Punctuating speech

If you write a story, your characters will talk to each other. If you write about a personal experience, you might put in the words that people said at the time. If you write a newspaper article, it will include the words any speakers said when they were interviewed. In all these situations, and more, you need to know how to punctuate speech.

Speech marks – which are sometimes called **quotation marks** or **inverted commas** – hover above a line of writing or printing. They go round the exact words a character or a real person says. Depending on the style of the book, newspaper or magazine, they can be single speech marks or come in pairs, and look like floating commas or apostrophes. In some handwriting and font styles, double speech marks can look like the numbers 66 and 99.

He asked, "Do we need anything for lunch?"

"You could buy a cake when you're out," she suggested.

"Excellent!" he said. "I'll get a chocolate one."

In this book, the style is to use single speech marks.

Group task

To be able to use speech marks properly, you need to be aware of which words are being said. This game will help you to do that.

One person from your group or class should say a short, simple sentence. After they have said it, they should pick someone else from the class, who has to repeat the sentence they just heard. Everyone else should listen carefully to check if the sentence has been properly and exactly repeated. Person two can now say a sentence of their own and then pick a third person who has to repeat it.

Remember, you are learning to focus on the exact words someone actually says. Keep going like this round the class. You can make it harder by speaking in longer and more complicated sentences.

>> Putting speech marks in the right places

In a cartoon or a graphic novel, the words someone says go in speech bubbles:

Have you seen my hat anywhere?

No!

That's odd. I thought I left it in the cupboard.

In written English, these words go inside speech marks:

> She said, 'Have you seen my hat anywhere?'
>
> 'No!' he snapped.
>
> 'That's odd,' she said. 'I thought I left it in the cupboard.'

 Building

Write out the sentences, putting **speech marks** in the right places. Everything else in the sentences is correct.

1   He asked, Do you have any apples?

2   The stallholder said, I have red ones, yellow ones and green ones.

3   He pointed at the red ones and asked, Are they for eating or cooking?

4   The stallholder answered, Eating. Did you want cooking apples?

5   He said, I want to bake an apple crumble.

Strengthening

Write out the sentences, putting **speech marks** in the right places. Everything else in the sentences is correct.

1   You want to use Bramleys, piped up a woman on the next stall.

2   Why? he asked.

3   They cook really well, she answered.

4   But I like Golden Delicious, he said.

5   You can't cook them. They'll go totally mushy, she told him.

Extending

Write out the sentences, putting **speech marks** in the right places. Everything else in the sentences is correct.

1   Wait a minute, said the greengrocer. Have you made a crumble before?

2   No, said the man, but I love eating them.

3   There's more to it than apples, said the woman. You can add brambles to make it more interesting.

4   But, said the man, I don't see any brambles on sale here.

5   That, said the stallholder, is because they grow wild. You'll have to pick them yourself.

Once you have checked your answers for the building, strengthening and extending tasks, look back at the three groups of sentences.

➤   In the **first** group, the speaker came first, then the words that they said. This is really clear, because we always know who is speaking, but it gets a little bit dull to keep reading lots of sentences that are written in the same way.

➤   In the **second** group, the spoken words came first, followed by the speaker. This can be more interesting, but the writer has to be careful not to confuse the reader. You can't use much speech before you say who's speaking, or the reader will get lost.

➤   In the **third** group, what each speaker said was broken up with some information about that speaker. This can be more interesting and varied, but it makes the other punctuation a little more complicated. (You will learn about that other punctuation on page 80.)

>> Using speech marks and paragraphs in conversations

When you have more than one person speaking, you need to use paragraph breaks to organise the conversation. If you don't do this, your stories will become horribly confusing.

Two rules will help you here:

When you change from one speaker to another, start a **new paragraph**.

Any words that tell you **about** the speaker go in the **same** paragraph as the words that the speaker says.

You can see both these rules being followed in this conversation:

> Ms Cooper told her pupils, 'I'd like you to use speech in your stories. It'll really make them come to life.'
>
> 'Can you remind us how to use them?' asked a girl from the back row.
>
> 'Of course,' said Ms Cooper. 'I'll put up a slide on the screen that explains how speech marks work.'

Mistake!

You can **never** have two sets of speech marks side by side. If you see something like this in your writing:

She said, 'I like your trainers.' 'Thank you,' he said.

then you can be sure you have missed out a paragraph break.

Your paragraph breaks for speech should look the same as all your other paragraph breaks. If you skip a line for a new paragraph, do that when you start a new paragraph for a new speaker. If you take a new line and **indent** your first words, do that when you start a new paragraph for speech. There is no different way of showing a new paragraph for speech.

 Crossover

You can find out more about how to use **paragraph breaks** and how to lay out **paragraphs** on pages 124–127.

Building

Write out this conversation, dividing it into **paragraphs** as you go. Everything else, including the speech marks, is correct.

> 'Excuse me,' said the reporter. 'What do you want?' asked the man. The reporter answered, 'Tell me about the rescue.' 'I have already spoken to Sky News,' said the man. 'I'm from the BBC,' said the reporter, holding up her ID. 'We have a lot more viewers and they really want to hear your story.' 'I'm not sure,' said the man. 'It's pretty emotional.'

 Strengthening

Write out this conversation, dividing it into **paragraphs** as you go. This time you will also need to add the speech marks, but everything else is correct.

> That's why it's so important, said the reporter, getting out her phone. OK, the man nodded. What do you want to know? When did you first know there was a problem? asked the reporter. The man stroked his beard thoughtfully. I got woken at 3 a.m. by the emergency alert on my phone. The call said a small fishing boat was in trouble on its way back in to shore. How did that make you feel? she asked. It's an adrenaline rush, he answered. You know you have to scramble. You know there are lives at risk.

Before you try an extending level task, here's one more important idea for you to think about.

If you paragraph your conversations properly, your paragraph breaks will guide the reader. A paragraph break shows that you are changing speaker, so you do not have to put the speaker's name, or some other 'tag' to identify them, in every paragraph. This lets you cut down on boring repetition of names. It makes your writing more stylish. It flows better and is more sophisticated.

 Extending

Write out the following conversation, dividing it into **paragraphs** and adding the **speech marks** as you go. This time you will also need to think carefully about who is speaking when, because the speech is not always 'tagged' with a name or person.

That sounds pretty intense, said the reporter. It is, he answered. When I go out on a rescue, I could save a life, or I might be too late. So what happened tonight? We all ran to the lifeboat station. How long did it take to get the crew assembled? Not long. Most of us live in the village, not far from the harbour. Everyone was there within five minutes and ready in ten. Some of us still had our pyjamas on under our waterproof suits. What was the mood like on the lifeboat? she asked, scribbling notes as he spoke. Surprisingly calm. We are well trained, and we were ready.

⤬ Crossover

There are many other reasons for using paragraph breaks. You will learn more about **paragraph breaks**, and about other reasons for dividing your writing into **paragraphs**, on pages 126–127.

›› How speech marks work with other punctuation

You already know the three most important rules for speech:

1   Put **speech marks** round the words someone says.

2   Start a **new paragraph** when you change who is speaking in a conversation.

3   Words that tell us about the speaker go in the **same paragraph** as the words the speaker says.

So far, we have not thought about any of the other punctuation that goes with speech. When we use speech marks, this also affects other punctuation marks nearby. We are going to add that to your knowledge now. We will build this up step by step, just as we did when you learned about ownership apostrophes on page 67.

› Step 1: using speech marks when the spoken words would end in ? or !

This is nice and easy. Question marks and exclamation marks never get changed. We keep them just the way they are, because we need them. They are there to show us something special about the sentence, as you learned on pages 57 and 60.

If the spoken words would start with a capital letter, that capital also stays as it is:

'Hang on!' I yelled, running to answer the knock on my door.

The delivery agent smiled at me and asked, 'Could you take a parcel for your neighbour?'

› Step 2: using speech marks when the spoken words would end in a full stop

This is a little trickier, depending on whether you are putting the speaker **before** or **after** the speech.

If you are **starting with the speaker**, the sentence that the speaker goes on to say gets to keep its full stop, which stays inside the closing speech marks. You should also use a comma just before the opening speech marks:

I answered, 'Of course, that's no problem.'

If you are **starting with the speech**, you end that speech with a comma, which sits inside the speech marks. You don't get to use a full stop until you have finished writing about the speaker at the end of your own sentence:

'Thank you,' said the delivery agent, handing me a form to sign.

Once again, if the spoken words would start with a capital letter, that capital stays as it is. You can see that in the examples above.

Using what you have learned from the explanations and examples in steps 1 and 2, write out these sentences. You can look back at the explanations and examples above to help you. Remember to:

➤ Put speech marks where they are needed.

➤ Use question marks and exclamation marks where they are needed.

➤ Use full stops and commas where they are needed.

➤ Use capital letters where they are needed.

1. what happened to your new trainers asked Scott's mum
2. he couldn't look her in the eye as he answered they fell in a muddy puddle and then a dog ran off with them
3. help yelled Andre as the lion turned towards him
4. the keeper raised her stun gun at the lion and shouted run
5. I really enjoyed that book said Martine
6. Rob added I love it too, and the film version is even better.
7. Marek added I think it's probably my favourite film
8. I thought the sequel was much better actually said Iwona

› Step 3: using the speech–speaker–speech pattern

This is the trickiest step of all, but if you can do this you can write really interesting and sophisticated sentences. In these sentences, you interrupt what the speaker says to tell the reader something about the speaker, like this:

‘I am absolutely sure,’ said a very shaky Andre, ‘that the lion wanted me for dinner.’

The words Andre says would be just one sentence:

‘I am absolutely sure that the lion wanted me for dinner.’

We end Andre's first bit of speech with a **comma**, because we haven't reached the end of his sentence.

We follow his name with another **comma**, because it introduces the second part of his interrupted speech. We end his speech with a **full stop** before the **speech mark**.

‘I am absolutely sure,’ said a very shaky Andre, ‘that the lion wanted me for dinner.’

Did that make sense? You can see the same pattern in the next sentence. The commas, speech marks and full stop have been picked out in red to help you notice them:

‘I believe,’ said the keeper, ‘that Leopold just wanted to come and play with you.’

If the speaker says two (or more) sentences, instead of just one interrupted one, you need a full stop before their second sentence, and it must start with a capital letter:

‘I don't agree,’ Andre insisted. ‘That beast had a really vicious look on its face.’

Using what you have learned about the speech–speaker–speech pattern from the explanations and examples on the previous page, write out these sentences. You can look back at the previous page's explanations and examples to help you. Remember to:

➤ Put speech marks where they are needed.

➤ Use question marks and exclamation marks where they are needed.

➤ Use full stops and commas where they are needed.

➤ Use capital letters where they are needed.

1 mr brown said the lawyer please tell the court who you saw that morning

2 well he gulped I looked out my window

3 why did you do that asked the lawyer what grabbed your attention

4 there was a noise in the street said mr brown looking nervously at the accused so I got up to see what was happening

5 and who did you see the lawyer asked again was it someone you can see in this courtroom today

6 yes said mr brown nervously I saw the man I can see standing in the dock

In this section of the book you have learned how to punctuate speech.

You have learned to put **speech marks** round the words someone says:

Ms Cooper smiled at her pupils and said, 'Well done. You worked hard.'

You have used **paragraph breaks** to organise conversations:

Ms Cooper smiled at her pupils and said, 'Well done. You worked hard.'

'I know we did,' said a boy at the front. 'You're really tough on us.'

You have learned how speech affects other punctuation marks like **full stops**, **question marks**, **exclamation marks** and **commas**:

'Cheeky!' said Ms Cooper. 'It's good for you.'

'I think,' said another pupil, 'that you're tough, but it's good for us anyway.'

You can show all that understanding now by completing the **Bringing it all together** revision task on the next page.

Bringing it all together

▶ Punctuating speech

Write out these sentences, putting speech marks in the right places. Everything else is correct.

1   Do you want to see a film on Saturday? he asked.

2   She nodded and said, Which one though?

3   I'm not sure, he said. What do you fancy: action or drama?

4   Action, she said. I love a good explosion.

5   I don't care what we see actually, he said, as long as we get loads of snacks.

6   All right, she agreed, but we're not having nachos. They smell terrible.

Divide this conversation into paragraphs, putting in speech marks as you go. Everything else is correct.

> What's the problem? asked the mechanic, pushing back her baseball cap as she peered into the engine. It's making a horrible noise. What kind of noise? Can you describe it? No, he said, but I can act it out for you. He tipped his head back and let out a heart-rending growl. OK, said the mechanic, I get the idea. So can you tell me what's up with my car? No, but I can tell you not to audition for a part in a musical.

Write out these sentences, using speech marks and other punctuation marks such as full stops, question marks, exclamation marks and commas where appropriate. The capital letters have been left in to give you some clues.

1   Wow said the antique dealer as he turned the vase over and over in his hands

2   What is it asked the owner

3   It's a magnificent piece he answered It's really old

4   She looked closer and asked Where do you think it's from

5   It might be Chinese he said which could make it old and valuable

6   How old How valuable Her eyes sparkled with excitement

7   Valuable enough that you should keep it in a bank vault he answered

8   Amazing She reached out a finger and gave the vase a stroke

▶ Commas

Our next punctuation mark is small, but it does a number of useful jobs for us.

A **comma** is a small, curly punctuation mark. It sits with its head on the line and its tail dangling down below.

Commas help us to navigate our way through sentences and can prevent confusion.

Commas are used for lists, to create small pauses in the structure of sentences, to build the technique called **parenthesis** and to help punctuate speech.

If you are typing your words, you should always have a space after a comma.

⤬ Crossover

You have already learned about how **commas** are used in **punctuating speech**. You can see that explained from page 81 onwards. In this part of the book, we will look at the other reasons for using commas.

❯❯ Using commas in lists

If a sentence contains a list, the items in that list are separated by commas:

I need eggs, butter, flour, sugar and cocoa powder to make the cake.

You don't need a comma before the final item, because the 'and' does the job of separating the last two items in the list.

Building

Write out these sentences, putting in the **commas** as you go.

1   I packed sunglasses a hat my sun cream and a book for the day at the beach.

2   They took juice crisps sausage rolls sandwiches and flapjacks for their picnic.

3   She needed a pencil rubber ruler and calculator for the maths exam.

4   It rained hailed snowed and blew a gale that day so we stayed at home.

5   When my car got stolen I lost my backpack a picnic blanket a kite and the shovel I keep in the boot in case of snow.

6   The shopping list reminded me to buy carrots bread apples salad leaves and lots of milk.

◄I—I► Strengthening

Write out these sentences, putting in the **commas** as you go.

1   The cast for the pantomime included a former reality TV star an ex-footballer an actor from a soap and a local radio presenter.

2   The head teacher's talk at assembly mentioned the school summer concert a rehearsal for the leavers' ceremony the problem with litter by the back entrance and a warning about speeding traffic near the front gate.

3   His outfit for the Oscars was made up of a well-cut suit beautifully polished black shoes a silk cummerbund and a fabulously vivid tie.

4   The superintendent told the press conference that the police were looking for a tall man with dark hair brown eyes a red football top white trainers and a pronounced limp in his left leg.

5   The aquarium had playful otters menacing sharks some extremely long eels a shoal of tiny clown fish and a tank full of lobsters who waved their claws at visitors.

6   The TV guide listed a police drama a soap a talent show for dogs a news bulletin and a travel show about Sydney.

So far in our use of commas in lists, the commas have just been there to keep the sentence tidy and organised. However, in some lists, those commas do a vital job in preventing confusion.

Look at this sentence and the picture below it.

> We spent the afternoon watching the rabbits on the lawn playing board games and reading.

Without commas, the sentence suggests an impossible picture. Some of the rabbits on the lawn are playing board games. Some of them are reading. That's ridiculous: rabbits can't read and they can't hold a dice or playing piece in their little paws.

Now look at what happens when we put just one comma into the sentence.

> We spent the afternoon watching the rabbits on the lawn, playing board games and reading.

Now we understand that some humans did three things on that relaxing afternoon. They watched the rabbits on the lawn. They played board games. They read.

 Extending

Below are two more sentences that need **commas** to create sense. For each sentence:

➤ First, draw a picture of what the sentence wrongly suggests when there are no commas.

➤ Then write out the sentence with commas in the right places to get it to make sense.

1 I enjoy cooking my dog and online gaming.

2 Our granny was fond of knitting her small flock of sheep and growing vegetables in her garden.

Sometimes a writer will dedicate a book to people they love or admire. Can you explain the difference between these two, quite similar, dedications?

➤ I dedicate this book to my parents, JK Rowling and Barack Obama.

➤ I dedicate this book to my parents, JK Rowling, and Barack Obama.

›› Using commas to create pauses in the structure of sentences

We can use commas to create short pauses in longer or more complex sentences. These pauses help us navigate our way through the sentence.

If we use commas correctly, we can write longer and more sophisticated sentences.

 Building

Look at this example:

> He walked slowly up to the house. He knocked on the door. He waited.

It is not a great piece of writing. All three sentences are short, and the repeated use of 'he' gets annoying. If we use commas, we can write something more interesting:

> He walked slowly up to the house, knocked on the door and waited.

The new longer sentence avoids repeating the **subject** of the sentence: 'he'. (You learned about subjects of sentences and verbs on page 18.) As you learned on page 85, you don't need a comma before the 'and'.

Following the example above, join the short sentences to make longer and more sophisticated ones. Remember to use **commas** and avoid repeating the subject of each sentence.

1 The bird spread its wings. It flew into the air. It landed on the highest branch of the tree.

2 I stepped forward. I opened the door of the car. I lifted out the baby in his car seat.

3 She put down her newspaper. She checked the time. She hurriedly got up to leave.

4 The vet filled the syringe. He stroked the horse. He carefully injected it with medicine.

5 We folded up our tent. We picked up our backpacks. We left our forest campsite.

6 A man across the road shouted at me. He waved his arms. He yelled a warning about the speeding car.

⫶⊩⫶ Strengthening

You can also use commas to help you write sentences in a different order. This sentence:

> We were happy to walk until it started raining.

could become:

> Until it started raining, we were happy walking.

Using a mix of sentence types – some like the first version, others like the second – will make your writing more varied and interesting.

Following the example above, reverse the order of the sentences to create variety. Remember to use a **comma** in the middle of each sentence.

1   We couldn't get out because a lorry had blocked the end of our driveway.

2   They lost everything in the flood except for the few things they could carry when they left the house.

3   He couldn't go out until he had finished all the housework.

4   The players stayed upbeat and cheerful despite losing the match.

5   It was dark that night because of the clouds although there was a full moon.

6   The band played lots of new material even though their fans would rather have heard their biggest hits.

Mistake!

What you **cannot ever** do is use a comma to join two separate sentences to each other just as they are, without changes. The sentences:

> **An oak is a very strong tree. Its wood is ideal for making beams for building houses.**

have to stay separate. You **cannot** write this:

> **An oak is a very strong tree, its wood is ideal for making beams for building houses.**

→

This mistake is called a **comma splice** because 'splice' is a word that means 'a join'. Commas just aren't strong enough to be used for making joins in this way. (You will soon learn about **colons** and **semi-colons**, which are stronger and can be used to join sentences together.)

You could write this:

> **An oak is a very strong tree, so its wood is ideal for making beams for building houses.**

because the conjunction 'so' is strong enough to make the join. (You learned about **conjunctions** on page 46.)

Read these sentences. The writer has wrongly used a comma splice. Use **conjunctions** to re-write the sentences, so that they are joined correctly.

1   I needed something for dinner, I went to the corner shop.
2   She liked Mars Bars best, she loved the layer of toffee under the chocolate.
3   I took her a card on her birthday, she always forgot mine.
4   We went there every summer, my parents didn't visit any more after I left home.
5   The cast stood at the front of the stage holding hands and bowing, the audience cheered and clapped.
6   The lights flickered and went out, the storm had brought the power lines down.

» Using commas to create parenthesis

Parenthesis is a technique that lets you drop extra information into a sentence.

Parenthesis can be made using a pair of commas:

> Ross, who had arrived late, slipped quickly into his seat.

The words between these commas add extra information to the sentence. If you took the information out, you would still have a meaningful sentence:

> Ross slipped quickly into his seat.

⤬ Crossover

You can also create parenthesis with a pair of **dashes** or with a pair of **brackets**. You will find out more about this on pages 102 and 105.

Write out these sentences, putting **commas** in the right places to create **parenthesis**. Remember that you always need to use a **pair** of commas, and that the sentence should still make sense if you remove the commas and the information that they enclose.

1   Benji the actor's trained meerkat made the audience roar with laughter.

2   The icing on the buns which had been sitting in the shop window all day had begun to melt and slide off.

3   My brother who has always been a bit spoiled just expects me to pay whenever we go out for lunch.

4   The drive took us three hours all of them rainy and boring and when we arrived the hotel had given our room to someone else.

5   The boat despite the hole that made it leak a little got safely into the harbour.

6   The toddler who was full of energy after his nap showed me all his favourite books and toys.

7   The writer after spending all day alone in her study had eaten nothing but chocolate biscuits and really needed to have something more nutritious.

8   Her playlist which she was sure she had chosen quite carefully seemed to be full of miserable songs about broken hearts.

There is a **Bringing it all together** revision task on the next page. Once you have done it, and your knowledge of commas is really strong, there is a little more to learn on the following page about two other uses of the comma.

Bringing it all together

▶ Commas

❭ Commas in lists

Write out these sentences, using commas in the right places.

1 The driver brought crates of milk boxes of biscuits cartons of pasta and bags of carrots to the supermarket.

2 The park was busy with people playing football and tennis having picnics walking dogs and sunbathing.

3 The bus was full of students tourists shoppers and grandparents taking children out for the day.

4 The case fell to the floor and popped open, spewing out clothes shoes toiletries books and a tangle of charger cables.

5 They planted poppies cornflowers dandelions daisies and marigolds in the wildflower meadow.

❭ Commas to create pauses and to structure sentences

Use commas to join these short sentences into longer, more fluent ones.

1 The baby clapped its hands. It dropped the teddy on the floor. It squealed.

2 The cyclist skidded to a halt. She threw her helmet on the ground. She groaned.

3 The mug crashed to the floor. It broke into pieces. It spilled coffee everywhere.

4 The builders knocked down the wall. They gathered up the bricks. They rolled them away in a wheelbarrow.

5 The singer stepped out on stage. She grabbed the microphone from its stand. She yelled, 'Hello, Edinburgh!'

❭ Commas to create parenthesis

Write out these sentences, using commas in the right places.

1 The dog which had been panting since the start of the walk drank the whole bowl of water in seconds.

2 The sun peeping out at last over the building opposite cast a splash of golden light across the garden.

3 Kenny having come to meet her sat and waited as she finished off her work.

>> Controversial commas

You now know the main ways that commas should be used. If you can follow what you have learned, your language will be clear and understandable.

There are two other ways that **some** writers use commas. These are controversial: other, equally skilled, writers would not use commas in these ways, because they believe that the way we use English has changed and evolved and that these commas are no longer needed.

> Commas between adjectives

When this writer was a hardworking, little girl she was taught to put tiny, little commas between all her wonderful, well-chosen adjectives. You can see what that would look like in the sentence you just read. (You learned about adjectives on page 8.)

Many writers would not do this now. They say that those commas don't add anything to the structure or the meaning, and that they make the page look fussy and cluttered:

> I found some lovely, old, shiny, black, patent, leather boots in a battered, ancient, heavy, oak trunk in an obscure, dusty corner of the attic.

> The Oxford comma

Look at this sentence, which you first met on page 86:

> We spent the afternoon watching the rabbits on the lawn, playing board games and reading.

The single comma does enough to get that sentence to make sense. That comma lets us know that the sentence is **not** about rabbits who enjoy a wee game of snakes and ladders and a Harry Potter story.

Some writers would add another comma to that sentence, just before the 'and':

> We spent the afternoon watching the rabbits on the lawn, playing board games, and reading.

This comma before the 'and' is called the Oxford comma. Some writers believe there should always be a comma before an 'and'. Others think, as they do about commas between adjectives, that using too many commas makes the page look cluttered.

The best response is to use an Oxford comma before 'and' **if, and only if, it helps make the language clearer**. This writer saw a sign on a bin that said:

> PLASTIC BOTTLES AND CANS

That's a bit confusing. Does it mean that any cans that go in the bin must be made of plastic? An Oxford comma would help to make clear what can be put in that bin:

93

> PLASTIC BOTTLES, AND CANS

although you could also make it clear by changing the word order, without using a comma at all:

> CANS AND PLASTIC BOTTLES

Good punctuation makes our language clear and understandable. It helps us to communicate better. If an Oxford comma makes your meaning clear, use it. If it doesn't create meaning, don't use it. If there is a neater way to be clear, do that instead.

 ## ▶ Colons

You learned on pages 89 and 90 that **commas** are not good at making strong connections. Using them to join sentences would be a **comma splice** and would be wrong. The next two punctuation marks you will meet are stronger; they can be used to make connections.

> A **colon** is made of two dots: the lower dot sits on the line with the upper dot above it.
>
> Colons have a number of uses: they can introduce a list, an explanation or an example, and they can also be used before quotations.
>
> If you look at the sentences above, you will see two colons, which are doing two of the jobs colons can do: the first one is introducing an explanation, the second introduces a list. In the sentence you have just read, the colon also introduces an explanation.

≫ Colons to introduce lists, explanations and examples

 Building

Write out these sentences, putting **colons** in the right places.

1   The librarian loved all kinds of books novels, encyclopaedias, biographies and even dictionaries.

2   I'm sorry I'm so late the bus broke down and I had to get out and walk.

3   I really don't like him he talks about himself all the time and doesn't care about anyone else.

4   There are lots of great places to visit in Barcelona my favourite is the cable car up to the Olympic park.

5 The rescue centre had all sorts of dogs waiting for homes terriers, collies, mongrels and even one that looked more like a wolf.

6 I'm feeling quite nervous I've never given a speech to such a big audience.

7 Scotland has produced many great writers Robert Burns is just one of many who are famous worldwide.

8 There's so much you could do on a wet Sunday afternoon bake a cake, catch up on your studies, get in touch with someone you haven't seen in a while or just do a bit of housework.

9 I looked a bit unprofessional I'd forgotten to put my work shoes in my bag and I had to go into the meeting wearing the trainers I put on to walk to the office.

10 The supermarket had run out of lots of things toilet rolls, pasta, flour and even peanut butter.

⫶—⫶ Strengthening

For each sentence you have just written out, decide what the **colon** was doing. Was it introducing:

➤ an example   ➤ a list   ➤ an explanation?

❯❯ Colons to introduce quotations

If you are writing an essay and want to quote from someone else's writing, you should introduce this quotation with a colon. It is also usual to put the quotation on a **new line**, inside quotation marks, and to **indent** it: to move it a little to the right. Look at this example:

> Shakespeare shows us that Romeo already feels he could not live without Juliet. When he sees her standing at her bedroom window, he says:
>
>   'Juliet is the sun.'
>
> All life on Earth would die without the sun. Romeo would die without Juliet.

These four actions together: using a colon, starting on a new line, using speech marks and indenting the quoted words are all there to help you to show clearly when you are writing in your own words and when you are quoting someone else's words.

How colons can affect sentences

Using, or not using, a colon can make a big difference to the meaning of a sentence. Look at this example:

> I'm afraid I don't like mice.

This is just someone saying, very politely, that they do not like those tiny, furry creatures.

Now look at what happens when we put a colon in the sentence:

> I'm afraid: I don't like mice.

The colon introduces the explanation of why this person might be cowering in the corner or standing on a chair shaking and shivering.

Explain the difference in meaning between the two versions below of the same sentence, with and without the colon.

> I'm sorry I'm allergic to nuts.   I'm sorry: I'm allergic to nuts.

⤨ Crossover

Some writers use dashes to do some of the jobs that colons can do. You will learn about using **dashes** on page 101. Generally, a dash feels quicker and more **informal**, whereas a colon feels stronger and more **formal**.

▶ Semi-colons

The semi-colon is an unusual punctuation mark. If you never use it, no one will mind or even notice, and you won't be wrong; if you can learn how to use it properly, you will seem very skilled.

A **semi-colon** is made of two marks, one above the other; the upper mark is a dot and the lower one is a comma.

Semi-colons make connections; they are used to join two sentences together when the sentences have closely connected ideas.

If you look at the sentences above, you will see two semi-colons. They are both doing the job this mark can do; they are joining sentences that are about very similar ideas. The first semi-colon is joining two sentences that are both about what a semi-colon looks like; the second semi-colon connects sentences that are both about connections.

 Group task

If you are working in a group or class, find a partner. Read the third, final, paragraph in the explanation box above. It contains two more **semi-colons** that are being used to join sentences.

You know that these sentences should be about closely connected ideas. Work out what the common idea is in each case. Be ready to explain your answer to the rest of your group or class.

❯❯ Using semi-colons to join sentences

Before you work on using semi-colons to join sentences, here's a little more explanation. A semi-colon can always be replaced **either** by a sentence break:

> Semi-colons make connections; they are used to join two sentences together.
>
> Semi-colons make connections. They are used to join two sentences together.

or by using the word 'and':

> He flung open the heavy old curtains; light flooded the dusty room.
>
> He flung open the heavy old curtains and light flooded the dusty room.

Remember: you will never be wrong if you don't use a semi-colon because there is always another way to do what a semi-colon does. These pages will teach you to be right when you do choose to use semi-colons, which will show that you are a skilled user of language.

You learned on pages 89-90 that you **can't** join sentences with commas; that creates the mistake called comma splice. A semi-colon is a kind of super-comma. It's a good compromise to use when a full stop would make sentences feel too cut off and separate, but when a comma would be too weak to make the join.

Building

Write out the following sentences, joining them correctly with **semi-colons**. HINT! You will need to change some capital letters into lower case ones.

1 He slipped on the pavement. It was very icy.

2 She turned on the tap. Rust-coloured water trickled out.

3 We visited London last summer. It is such a crowded city.

4 I went back to college that autumn. I wanted to pass more exams.

5 The car came clattering to a noisy halt. They'd let the petrol tank run dry.

6 Almost £500 appeared in my bank account today. I got my money back for the flights that the airline cancelled.

Strengthening

Write out the following sentences, joining them correctly with **semi-colons**. This time you also need to put in capital letters and full stops. Remember, the words on each side of the semi-colon must be capable of being a sentence.

1 although he doesn't train very hard he is good at rugby he got picked for the team

2 we are going to the fair at the weekend the waltzers and dodgem cars arrived at the park yesterday

3 the imam from our mosque won first prize in the bake-off he made a cake flavoured with rosewater and cinnamon

4 I'm miserable and exhausted I've been looking for our cat all day and I can't find her

5 I couldn't concentrate on my work during the train journey the passenger in the seat next to me was eating some very crunchy crisps

Extending

These sentences have been joined with conjunctions. (Look back at page 46 if you want a reminder of what those are.) Re-write the sentences, joining them correctly with **semi-colons** instead. HINT! You will need to remove or add some words, so that you can be sure you have a complete sentence on each side of the semi-colon.

1 We loved the film because it was about monsters lurking in a disused building.

2 I was determined to reach the summit alone and without ropes as this was my greatest ambition.

3   Because the winter was long and severe the army delivered animal food to snowed-in farms.

4   The remaining workers left and the gates were locked behind them as the factory shut down at last.

5   I gave up practising the guitar because it wasn't worth playing after the band broke up.

>> Using semi-colons to organise complicated lists

You learned about using commas in lists on page 85. Commas are really useful for joining simple items in lists:

> I packed sunglasses, a hat, my sun cream and a book.

Sometimes a list is made up of longer, more complicated items. Those items might need their own commas already. Imagine you were going off on an expedition and needed:

> a waterproof jacket with a hood, deep pockets and a removable fleece lining
>
> strong, light walking boots that were not too expensive
>
> tasty, nutritious food that was easy to carry and quick to prepare

When you have a complex list like this, semi-colons can help you to organise the separate items. You could turn the list into one sentence, like this:

> I gathered and checked my equipment: a waterproof jacket with a hood, deep pockets and a removable fleece lining; strong, light walking boots that were not too expensive; tasty, nutritious food that was easy to carry and quick to prepare.

Did you notice that the sentence began with a short opening phrase to let us know what the whole sentence is about, and the list was introduced with a colon? Read the sentence again, making sure you can see those things.

Read the two lists below. Use them to create sentences like the one above. Make sure you use an opening phrase and a colon, as well as semi-colons between the items on the list.

List 1	List 2
a handbag containing a purse, keys and an out-of-date bus pass	a cute, scruffy puppy with a white body and brown tail
a very expensive, brand new mobile phone	a guinea pig called Mr Snuggles
a pile of photographs, all of the same child but at different ages	a grumpy, old Siamese cat
	a hibernating tortoise with a mottled green and brown shell

Bringing it all together

▶ Colons and semi-colons

❭ Colons to introduce lists, explanations and examples

Write out these sentences, using colons where they are needed.

1   She took very little when she left for university her three favourite books, a pile of clothing, a mug with her name on it and three packets of emergency cookies.

2   I would hate to go to Mars it's such a long way and the scenery would be boring.

3   Steven Spielberg has made many great films *Bridge of Spies* and *The BFG* are just two of them.

4   He knew lots about China his grandparents lived in Shanghai and he had often gone there to visit them.

5   It was an odd line-up for a car race two ancient Minis, a battered old Porsche, a sleek silver Rolls Royce and a muddy Land Rover.

❭ Semi-colons to join sentences

Write out these sentences, using semi-colons where they are needed.

1   A semi-colon is a useful punctuation mark it lets you join short sentences to make longer, more fluent ones.

2   The actor's house was full of glittering awards she had won three Oscars, a Golden Globe and two BAFTAs.

3   It rained for two days without stopping many roads were closed by flooding and a bridge washed away.

4   The wizard pointed his wand and yelled an incantation the lion froze in mid-air just out of range.

5   She had bought a random assortment of shopping none of it was very nutritious but some of it looked really tasty.

❭ Semi-colons to organise complicated lists

Write out this sentence, using semi-colons where they are needed.

I set up my home office with a supportive, adjustable desk chair some sturdy, white cardboard filing boxes for all my papers a brand new cork pinboard above my desk to stick notes on and an adjustable silver lamp to light up my workspace.

▶ Dashes and hyphens

We are going to deal with the next two marks together, because they look very similar. Despite that likeness, they do different, and almost opposite, jobs for us.

> Each of these marks looks like a tiny line, hovering above the line on the page.
>
> A **dash** is a little bit longer, and there are **spaces** before and after it. Dashes are used to keep words and ideas **apart**:
>
> > Samir – who was dressed as a decomposing cupcake covered in cockroaches – won the prize for best Halloween costume.
>
> A **hyphen** is a little bit shorter, with **no space** before or after. Hyphens are used to **join** words or to show that parts of words that have been split ought to be **joined together**:
>
> > They had long-term plans to shoot their latest blockbuster movie on the Florida coast, but a devastating category-three hurricane destroyed the beach where they intended to film.

Write out this passage. Each time you come to one of the numbers, decide if you need a **dash** to keep words **apart** or a **hyphen** to **join** them together. There are deliberate spaces around all the brackets, so you won't get any clues from how the words have been spaced out on the page.

> I've always **(1)** ever since I was a tiny child **(2)** been very short **(3)** sighted. This can cause all kinds of problems. I risk eating out **(4)** of **(5)** date food because I can't read the small print on the labels.
>
> Sometimes **(6)** despite careful efforts **(7)** I make mistakes. A man **(8)** eating shark I spotted in the sea just off Cornwall turned out **(9)** to my shame **(10)** to be a playfully leaping dolphin and the splash of ruby **(11)** red blood I thought I'd seen in the water was just a beachball it was playing with. The local news programme **(12)** which has told plenty whoppers of its own over the years **(13)** accused me of spreading a made **(14)** up rumour just to get publicity.

›› Other uses for dashes

You know already that dashes are used to keep words apart, and there are always spaces before and after them.

It's time to learn a little more about how dashes work. This ties in with a lot of what you have already learned about some other punctuation marks.

⤫ Crossover

On page 90 you learned about using pairs of **commas** to form **parenthesis**. The commas enclose extra information that you could get rid of while still having a complete sentence.

Pairs of dashes can also be used to create parenthesis in exactly the same way:

> Parenthesis – which is a clever little writing technique – can be made using commas, dashes or brackets.

⤫ Crossover

On page 94 you learned about using **colons** to introduce a list, an explanation or an example.

Many writers nowadays use a single dash in the same way as a colon:

> He left everything behind – his keys, his phone, even his wallet with his money and ID.

> I don't like cooked mushroom – it looks like little slices of slug.

> I love all the Marvel movies – *Black Panther* is my favourite.

Not all writers or teachers would agree with using a dash instead of a colon in this way. It definitely feels more **informal** and perhaps a bit more rushed. It is often a better choice to use the more traditional and **formal** colon rather than using this kind of speedy, chatty dash.

A dash can also create a **pause** in a sentence, getting the reader to wait just a tiny moment before they go on to your next thought or idea:

> None of my other friends liked him at all – I thought he was amazing.

Not all writers or teachers would agree with using a dash in this way. In this kind of example, it would be slightly more **formal** and correct to use a semi-colon instead:

> None of my other friends liked him at all; I thought he was amazing.

›› Other uses for hyphens

You know already that hyphens are used to join words together, and there are no spaces before or after them.

It's time to learn a little more about how hyphens work.

Because hyphens join words together, they are really useful in helping us to avoid confusion.

Look at these two sentences:

> I saw a man-eating chicken in that restaurant by the marketplace.

> I saw a man eating chicken in the restaurant by the marketplace.

The only difference in the writing is that there is a hyphen in the first sentence, but not in the second. However, the two sentences have very different meanings.

➤ The first sentence tells us the speaker saw a chicken at the restaurant. The chicken was so savage and vicious that it was eating a man.

➤ The second sentence tells us the speaker saw a man having some food. The man was not eating pork, or lamb, or beef; the man was eating chicken.

 Group task

Look at these two sentences:

I bought some extra, thick cream.   I bought some extra-thick cream.

Can you explain the difference in their meanings? If you are working in a class or group, work out the answer with a partner and be ready to explain it to the rest of the class. If you are using this book alone, write down an explanation, or draw two cartoons to show the difference in the two meanings.

There is one more very specific job that hyphens can do for us. We use them when we cannot quite fit a long word on one line of writing or printing and have to continue the word on the next line:

> Hyphens are tiny but powerful, like many of the other punc-
> tuation marks that you have learned about in this book.

If you use a hyphen in this way, you must break the word between two of its syllables. You only need to use one hyphen, and it goes at the end of the upper line:

Her bag was so full of apples and oranges that it was pra⁻ˣ
ctically bursting at the seams.

Her bag was so full of apples and oranges that it was prac
ˣ⁻tically bursting at the seams.

Now that you have learned about dashes and hyphens, there are just two more punctuation marks to go. Once you have learned about them, you will find the last of our **Bringing it all together** revision tasks at the end of the chapter.

▶ Brackets

Brackets are thin, curved marks that stand up on the line. They **always** come in pairs.

Brackets are used to separate information, ideas and details from the rest of the sentence:

Many people believe that Britain won the Second World War **(**1939–1945**)** because of Winston Churchill's strong leadership.

They took maps, a picnic and the dog **(**of course**)** for their walk in the hills.

The words inside the brackets give extra detail or information that you could remove without changing the meaning of the sentence.

 Building

Write out the sentences, adding the other **bracket** to complete the pair.

1   William Wallace (who was played by Mel Gibson in the film *Braveheart* won the Battle of Stirling Bridge in 1297.

2   After my old bike which was almost worn out anyway) got stolen, I got a new, much better, one.

3   She felt really homesick (an emotion she had never experienced before during her gap year.

4   Their increased support during the election when they won 56 per cent of the vote) brought the party into power for the first time.

5   The children in the garden (who were just enjoying being outdoors after days of rain were making so much noise that I couldn't hear the TV.

Strengthening

Write out the sentences, adding **brackets** where they are needed.

1   Aaron's favourite mug which he'd had since it came as a free gift with a childhood Easter egg fell to the floor and smashed into pieces when the cat jumped up on the table.

2   The kitchen floor never that clean at the best of times was now covered in a thin layer of coffee.

3   The cat seeing the delicious puddle of milky liquid jumped down again and started licking up the puddles of coffee with its slim, agile tongue.

4   Aaron's flatmate Ben having heard the crash as the mug hit the floor wandered in to see what was going on.

5   Aaron and the cat watched both with equally embarrassed expressions on their faces as Ben got a mop from the cupboard and started cleaning up.

>> Using brackets to make parenthesis

 Crossover

On page 90 you learned about using pairs of **commas** to form **parenthesis** and on page 102 you learned about making parenthesis by using pairs of **dashes**. The commas or dashes enclose extra information that you could get rid of while still having a complete sentence.

You can also create parenthesis by using pairs of brackets:

Parenthesis (which you have been learning about throughout this chapter) can be made using commas, dashes or brackets.

Pairs of commas create quite a gentle parenthesis. The information inside the commas is not very cut off from the rest of the sentence, because it matters quite a lot to the meaning of the sentence:

Fiona, a generous person, supported a number of local charities.

Pairs of dashes create a stronger-feeling parenthesis:

She set aside money from her wages each month – which was sometimes quite a sacrifice – to support the causes she believed in.

A parenthesis made of brackets feels like the strongest of all, with the words inside the brackets most cut off from the rest of the sentence, perhaps because those words matter least to the meaning or message of that sentence:

Her favourite charity (which met in a workshop next to the canal) helped lonely older men to learn woodworking skills as a way of spending time together.

▶ Slashes

It's time to meet our last punctuation mark.

A **slash** is a thin line. It looks as if it is falling over towards the right of the page:

A slash can be used in the expression 'and/or':

Pupils and/or staff should sign in at the office if visiting the building during school holidays.

and that is actually a good summary of what a slash does, because slashes suggest alternatives and choices:

tea/coffee £1.50

Not all writers or teachers would agree with using a **slash** in these ways. A slash can feel **informal** and rushed. It is often more effective to use the word 'or' rather than a slash.

No dogs/bikes in playground

No dogs or bicycles in the playground.

Slashes are sometimes used by writers who are trying to avoid being sexist:

Dear Sir/Madam   If the manager is in, s/he should answer any queries.

Again, not every writer would agree with this. In the first example, if you are being so **formal** that you are starting a letter with words like 'Sir' and 'Madam', you should be completely formal and write:

Dear Sir or Madam

using a word instead of a slash.

In the second example, if a person's gender is unknown, or irrelevant, it is better to use 'they':

If the manager is in, they should answer any queries.

It doesn't matter if the manager is female or male. The only thing that is important is whether they are able to answer the queries people have for them.

Read the following phrases and sentences. Decide if you think that the writer was correct to use a slash.

➤ If you agree with the writer, write the number and a tick in your jotter.

➤ If you disagree with the writer, re-write the language to get rid of the slash.

HINT! When you are getting rid of slashes, you may also need to make other small changes to the writing.

1 juice/water £1

2 Clients with dogs/cats/rabbits should attend the Monday pet clinic; those with guinea pigs/gerbils/hamsters should come on Tuesdays.

3 Only a passport and/or valid driving licence will be accepted as proof of identity.

4 A good teacher will know his/her pupils' needs and plan lessons to suit them.

5 Sprinkle the chocolate chips and/or chunks of toffee on top of the cake just before you put it in the oven.

6 Painter/decorator wanted for immediate start on various local jobs.

7 Use yellow and/or orange paint to suggest the sunset and dark blue for the sea.

8 If a police officer is first on the scene of a traffic accident, s/he should make sure that an ambulance has been called for.

The most common reason for using a slash is one you will probably never have to write out for yourself. Slashes appear in the full version of web addresses:

https://www.hoddergibson.co.uk

but if you ever type a web address at all, you probably only type the short form:

www.hoddergibson.co.uk

which takes you to the same place anyway.

Bringing it all together

▶ Dashes, hyphens, brackets and slashes

First, using your knowledge of these four punctuation marks, decide if each of the following sentences is **TRUE** or **FALSE**.

Next, for every sentence that is **FALSE**, write a short note for yourself to explain why this is the case.

1   A dash is shorter than a hyphen.

2   Slashes are useful in helping us to write formally.

3   You can use dashes to create parenthesis.

4   Hyphens can show where a word has been broken across two lines.

5   Hyphens keep words and ideas apart.

6   It is all right to use 'they' if you do not know the gender of the person you are writing about.

7   A man-eating tiger is safe.

8   A hyphen is longer than a dash.

9   Any words inside brackets are vital to the meaning of a sentence.

10   Some writers use dashes to suggest a pause in a sentence.

11   There are no spaces around hyphens.

12   A parenthesis made of brackets is the weakest type of parenthesis.

13   Dashes have spaces before and after them.

14   You can use a bracket on its own.

15   Dashes keep words and ideas apart.

16   A man eating tiger has unusual tastes.

17   If you don't type the slashes in a web address, your device won't find the website.

18   It is perfectly all right to use dashes as you would colons – to introduce a list, explanation or example.

3 Sentences and paragraphs

So far in this book, you have learned about parts of speech – the different types of words in our language – and about the punctuation marks we use when we put those words together to make sentences. In this chapter you will learn more about what makes a good sentence and how to put sentences together into paragraphs. We'll start all of that by looking at how we start every sentence.

▶ Capital letters

Capital letters are sometimes called upper case letters. When papers and books were printed using actual metal letters, printers needed a way to organise those bits of metal to get at them quickly. They used wooden cases, with slots for each letter. The capital letters were kept in the upper case, and the other ones went in the lower case.

Capital or upper case letters are used for a number of reasons. The two most common reasons are to show the start of a sentence:

> It's a beautiful day today.

or to start a proper noun, which is the name of a particular person or place:

> While he was visiting his relations in Egypt, Abdul enjoyed a trip to Cairo.

⤬ Crossover

Because capital letters are so common, they appear in many other parts of this book. On page 4 you can learn about using capital letters for **proper nouns**. On page 54 you can see how they are used in **interjections**. From page 55 onwards you can practise using them in **sentences** that end with **full stops**, **question marks** or **exclamation marks**. And, on page 81, you can learn about how capital letters are used when we punctuate **speech**.

We will not go over these ideas again here; you can look back at those other areas of the book whenever you need to. You will also have another chance to practise using capital letters when we learn about sentences on page 112.

 **Building**

Capital letters are used for proper nouns – the names of particular people or places.

1   Write a list of the last ten people you spoke to, using **capital letters** for their names. HINT! You may know some of those people by a title, such as Ms or Dr; those titles also take capital letters.

2   Now write a list of ten places you could reach within a ten-minute walk of where you are sitting and that have names which are proper nouns that would begin with a **capital letter**. HINT! If it is difficult to think of ten places to walk to, try this task again with places you could drive to in less than ten minutes.

›› Other reasons for using capital letters

As well as for proper nouns and at the start of sentences, we use capital letters for a number of other reasons.

As you read through the list of reasons, try to think of three more examples for each way that we use capital letters: three more titles, three more months, three more companies and so on.

We use capital letters:

➤   for the **titles** of books, films, plays and other creative works:

The funniest play Shakespeare wrote was *Twelfth Night*.

The Picasso painting *Guernica* shows the artist's feelings about war.

➤   for **days** of the week and **months** of the year:

I haven't been to the office since the first Monday in March.

➤   for the names of **organisations** and **companies**:

the Royal College of Physicians   Amazon   Tesco

➤   for the names of educational and medical **institutions**:

the University of Edinburgh   the Queen Elizabeth Hospital

➤   for **brand** names:

Apple   Nike   Mars   Starbucks   Renault

➤   when the single letter 'I' is used as word:

He asked if I would rather have tea or coffee.

➤   for some **abbreviations**:

BBC   UK

➤   for **countries**, **nationalities** and **languages**:

People in France speak French; most Mexican people speak Spanish.

➤ You can see in the examples above that we usually don't bother with capitals in tiny words like 'and', 'the', 'a', 'of' and so on, unless they are the first word in a **title**:

Of Mice and Men   *The Merchant of Venice*

 Building

In this passage, the capital letters are correct at the start of each sentence and in some other places too. However, they are missing in the proper nouns, the titles, and the days and months, as well as nationalities and languages.

Write out the passage, changing lower case letters into **capitals** as you go. HINT! Don't worry if you haven't heard of some of these places and people: the passage has enough clues to help you work out which words need capitals.

> Wherever I go in the world, I try to visit an art gallery. Last april I went to madrid. The prado museum has some amazing pictures, and if you visit after 5 p.m. on a sunday it's free to get in. The most famous painting is called las meninas, and it's by velázquez. It's a picture of the royal family, and the artist has put himself in the painting too. I didn't understand the title, because I can't speak spanish, but a museum guard (who was actually croatian) told me that it has something to do with the servants you can see in the picture.

Strengthening

In this passage, the capital letters are correct at the start of each sentence and in some other places too. However, they are missing in the proper nouns, the titles, and the days and months. They have also been missed from the names of organisations, companies and institutions.

Write out the passage, changing lower case letters into **capitals** as you go. HINT! Again, the passage has enough clues to help you work out whether any unfamiliar words need capitals.

> Next june I plan to go to paris to look at the pictures in the louvre, though I won't be able to visit on a tuesday, when it's always closed. Their most famous picture is leonardo's mona lisa, which is probably the best-known painting in the world.
>
> The best thing is, I won't even have to pay for my trip. Every time I shop in tesco I get customer points. I save them up and use them to pay for free flights with air france. I can spend my points on hotels too. I've found a really nice-looking one near the river seine and the eiffel tower. I might even get a discount on the louvre itself if I show them my membership card for the international association of museum curators.

Extending

In this passage, the capital letters are correct at the start of some sentences. However, they are missing in the proper nouns, the titles, and the days and months. They have also been missed from the names of organisations, companies and institutions. The writer has even forgotten to use them for the word 'I' and for abbreviations and brand names.

Write out the passage, changing lower case letters into **capitals** as you go. HINT! Again, the passage has enough clues to help you work out whether any unfamiliar words need capitals.

> i've wanted to visit the museum of modern art in new york ever since i saw a programme about it on the bbc years ago. It's right in the heart of manhattan, just off fifth avenue. Even if you only have an hour to spend there, you could see van gogh's the starry night and broadway boogie woogie by mondrian, which looks like a streetmap made of yellow and red lines.
>
> i had much more than an hour for my visit: i had the whole day. By the time i reached the end i was exhausted. i staggered to the nearest burger king and ordered myself a whopper with extra fries and a diet coke. Nobody can be highly cultured and classy all the time.

▶ Sentences

All of our written language is made up of sentences.

> A sentence is a sequence of words that make sense, on their own, together. Every sentence begins with a **capital letter**. Most sentences end with a **full stop**:
>
> We went to the station in a taxi.
>
> Some sentences end with a question mark:
>
> How much does a taxi to the station cost?
>
> Sentences sometimes end with an exclamation mark:
>
> Stop that taxi!

It is not the capital letter and the full stop (or the question or exclamation mark) that make words into a sentence. The capital and the full stop show that those words are already a sentence; it is the words themselves that make the sentence. Those words have to make sense, on their own, together. If the words don't make sense together, you have not written a sentence.

Building

Read the sequences of words. If they would work as a **sentence**, write them out, using a capital letter at the start and a full stop, question mark or exclamation mark at the end. If the words would not work as a sentence, just write X in your jotter.

1	help me	2	we met by the bridge	3	next to the library
4	after spending an hour at the pool	5	where is the car	6	down by the bridge
7	as cold as ice	8	I spent an hour at the pool	9	where the car is
10	it's next to	11	it is ice cold	12	to help me

Let's remind ourselves of our definition:

A sentence is a sequence of words that make sense, on their own, together.

 Crossover

Every sentence needs a **verb**. Without a verb, a sequence of words cannot make sense and will never be a sentence. You learned about verbs on page 18 of this book.

Look back at the sentences you just wrote down. Underline the **verb** in each one. HINT! Remember that the verb of being is extremely irregular. Look back at page 24 if you would like a reminder about this tricky verb.

 Strengthening

Write out each group, dividing it into **sentences** as you go by working out where to put **capital letters**. End each sentence with a **full stop**, a **question mark** or an **exclamation mark**, as appropriate. Underline the **verbs**.

1 listen I'm sorry, but you can't have a picnic here you are far too close to the edge of the cliff, and it's just not safe use one of the picnic tables over there instead

2 i'm not sure what to do at the weekend my friend Hannes is over from Germany for a few days there's a band playing in the park on Saturday should we go to hear them

3 i spent some time yesterday watching a bird on my kitchen window ledge the bird was small and brown it was too big to be a wren was it a sparrow it sang loudly i think I will leave some seeds out the bird might come back

4 my neighbour is exercising in his garden he just did 20 press-ups before that, he lifted a pair of dumb-bells, switching between his left and right arms now he's admiring himself in the screen of his phone and taking selfies he has no idea that I can see him

5   at first, the sound was almost too quiet to hear something rustled through the leaves something snapped tiny twigs and snuffled as it scampered the creature came closer, moving faster and more confidently finally, it emerged into the clearing

 Crossover

There is another, quite similar, exercise on page 63, in the part of the book that deals with **full stops**, **question marks** and **exclamation marks**. If you haven't done that exercise already, you could do it now as further sentence practice.

 Extending

Here are the skeletons of eight sentences. Copy them out, adding suitable words wherever you see an ellipsis. Use **capital letters**, **full stops**, **question marks** and **exclamation marks** wherever they are needed.

1   It was dark and quiet in …

2   Suddenly I heard …

3   I didn't know whether to …

4   … and everyone else in the house …

5   … tiptoed …

6   … a light …

7   My legs shook and …

8   As I … the door, I saw …

 Group task

For this task, you need some loose paper to write on, not your jotter.

First, write at least **five** sentences. Don't let anybody else see what you write. Each sentence should be between **five** and **ten** words long. Skip a couple of blank lines after each sentence.

Now, cut out your sentences, so that each one becomes a separate strip of paper.

Then, cut each sentence into two parts. Decide the best place to split each sentence. Make the cuts very neat and vertical so the shape doesn't give any jigsaw clues.

Next, swap your broken sentences with someone else. Put each other's sentences back together.

Finally, compare your answers. Did you put the sentences back together in the way your partner wrote them? If you found a different way of joining the halves, were they still correct sentences? If you found a different way of joining them, were the new sentences more interesting?

›› Sentence types

Most sentences tell us some information or an opinion. They are called statements:

> My new car is blue.   My new car is wonderful.

Some sentences ask something. They are called questions:

> What kind of car did you buy?

Some sentences tell us what to do. They are called commands or instructions:

> Park the car over there.

Some, very rare, sentences break the rules, because they don't have a verb. They only make sense because we understand the context. They are called minor sentences:

> Nice car!

All of the sentences above were about a car. To show your understanding of sentence types, make up each of the four types of sentence – a statement, a question, a command and a minor sentence – about each of these four ideas:

➤ a dog ➤ some money ➤ a boy ➤ some milk

HINT! The key word has to appear in every sentence, just as 'car' is in every example sentence above. You can look at those examples again to help you.

›› The structure of a sentence

If you cannot write good sentences, your writing will not make sense. Readers will not understand you, and you will not be able to express your ideas.

You can write good sentences by doing what we have learned already: start with a **capital letter**; write a sequence of words that make sense together; end with a **full stop**, a **question mark** or an **exclamation mark**.

If you follow these rules, you will make sense and write well.

You can choose now to add to your sentence knowledge by learning about **why** sentences make sense and **how** sentences are built up and put together. Lots of excellent writers don't know why their sentences are good; they just write good sentences. Lots of excellent writers would not be able to use words like predicate. What you are about to learn is interesting, but it isn't essential for your writing. However, it can be very useful in helping you to read and analyse someone else's writing, which is a skill that is often tested in exams.

❯ Sentence structure step 1: subjects and predicates

🔀 Crossover

You learned on page 18 that every sentence needs a **verb**. Every verb has a **subject** – the person or thing that does the verb. We're going to build on that knowledge now.

Every sentence can be split into two parts. One part of a sentence is the **subject**. The other part – all of the rest of the sentence, including the verb – is called the **predicate**. Look at the examples below. The verbs are in italic.

Subject	Predicate
We	*got up* far too late today.
The cat	*is playing* with some scraps of torn paper.
The coach	*praised* the players at half-time.
They	*will move to* Aberdeen next year.

🔨 Building

Write out the sentences. Draw a bubble round each **subject**. Underline the **verbs**.

1 The band's music was incredibly loud.

2 The swans on the pond had at least seven tiny, fluffy cygnets.

3 My cheese scones refused to rise and came out of the oven like leather.

4 Wax gets very hot as it melts.

5 The frustrated driver had to call a mechanic.

Strengthening

Here are some **subjects**. Write them out and add interesting **predicates** to complete the sentences. Write **at least five** words for each predicate. Underline your **verbs**.

1 The cute toddler …

2 An unexpected rainstorm …

3 My dad's older brother …

4 The reality TV star …

5 Two enormous tree trunks …

Here are some **predicates**. Add interesting **subjects** before each one to complete the sentences. Write **at least three** words for each subject. Underline the **verbs**.

1   ... was extremely hard work.

2   ... wanted to ride the biggest, fastest rollercoaster.

3   ... is visiting this country for the very first time.

4   ... jumped out from behind the door.

5   ... was the best that I had ever seen in my life.

❯ Sentence structure step 2: subjects, verbs and objects

You have just learned that every sentence can be split into two parts. One part is the **subject** – the person or thing that does the verb. All of the rest of the sentence, including the verb, is called the **predicate**.

We can unpack the predicate a little bit more. The predicate is the chunk of the sentence that contains both the **verb** and also the object of that verb (if there is one). The object is the person or thing that the verb is done to. Let's look at some of the examples you saw before. The verb is in italic, and the object is in bold.

Subject	Predicate
The cat	*is playing* with **some scraps of torn paper**.
The coach	*praised* **the players** at half-time.

Every sentence has a subject and a predicate. Every predicate contains a verb, but not all verbs have objects. Verbs don't have to happen **to** something or someone. Some verbs are intransitive. They just happen. Look at this sentence:

Dogs run.

The subject is 'Dogs' and the predicate is 'run'. The verb does not have an object. Running is just a thing that dogs do. In this sentence, 'run' is an intransitive verb.

Now look at this sentence:

Dogs run after balls.

The subject is 'Dogs' and the predicate is 'run after balls'. The verb has an object: 'balls'. It is the balls that have some running done to them. In this sentence, 'run' is a transitive verb.

 Crossover

You learned about transitive and intransitive verbs on pages 26–27. You can look back at those pages if you need a reminder.

Building

Write out the sentences below. Underline the **verb** in each one. If the verb has an **object**, draw a bubble round it.

1   Haunting music wafted out.

2   Peacocks scream noisily and often.

3   Sentence structure is complicated.

4   Sentence structure is hurting my brain.

5   I hurried to answer the ringing doorbell.

6   Her feet crunched the broken glass on the workshop floor.

7   Athletes train hard and often before any major competition.

8   Their coach trained the athletes before the competition.

Strengthening

Write **at least five** simple sentences of your own. Each sentence must have a **subject** and a **predicate**. Make sure that each predicate includes both a **transitive verb** and the **object** of that verb.

If you are working in a group or class, skip two lines in your jotter after each sentence, so that you can do the **extending** task below.

 Extending – group task

If you are working in a group or a class, find a partner. Swap jotters, and read the sentences your partner wrote for the **strengthening** task above. In each sentence:

➤   draw a bubble round the subject

➤   underline the **verb** with a straight line

➤   underline the **object** with a wiggly line.

› Sentence structure step 3: clauses and sentences

A clause is a group of words that includes a main verb and its subject.

A main clause is a clause that can work on its own as a sentence:

> I love drinking coffee.

A subordinate clause still has a verb and subject but does not work on its own as a sentence:

> as I walk to work

You can join subordinate clauses to main clauses to make sentences. These are called multiple or complex sentences:

> I love drinking coffee as I walk to work.

 Building

Write out these **multiple sentences**. Underline the **main clause** in each one. HINT! Remember that a main clause would be able to work as a sentence on its own.

1   If she has time, she will visit her granny tomorrow.

2   After the party finished, they walked home through the summer dusk.

3   Haunting music wafted out of the church, filling the air with voices.

4   When they are trying to attract a mate during springtime, peacocks scream noisily and often.

5   Sentence structure is complicated and makes my brain hurt.

6   I hurried to answer the ringing doorbell, tripping over a bag I'd left lying on the hall floor.

7   Their feet crunched the broken glass on the workshop floor, giving away their position to the trackers following them.

8   Because they so desperately want to win, athletes train hard and often before any major competition.

Strengthening

Add a **subordinate clause** to each main clause to make a **multiple sentence**. HINT! Remember that a subordinate clause should not be able to stand as a sentence on its own, but that the clause does still need a **verb** and a **subject**.

1   I walked along the empty high street ...

2   They picked armloads of apples ...

3   ... he became quite grumpy.

4   I got there as quickly as I could ...

5   ... our dog needs a trip to the grooming parlour.

6   ... she turned away, ignoring him.

You now know about main and subordinate clauses, and you know that every sentence needs a main clause. You know that subordinate clauses have to be joined to main clauses to make sense, and this creates what we call a multiple or complex sentence.

There's one more kind of sentence for you to learn about: compound sentences. If we join two main clauses together, that is called a compound sentence.

> ### ⤫ Crossover
>
> A compound sentence is a sentence with two (or more) main clauses. From page 46 onwards, you learned about conjunctions and how they can be used to join short sentences together to make longer and more sophisticated sentences. Those short sentences became the main clauses in your new, longer, compound sentences.

Read this list of main clauses:

A   I fell out of a tree

B   I prepared really carefully for the interview

C   I bought myself a sports car

D   My neighbour grew up on a tiny farm on a remote island

E   Someone in my street is loudly practising the bagpipes

F   I like chocolate with nuts or toffee in it

Now look at this list of conjunctions:

➤ and   ➤ so   ➤ but

We can use the main clauses and conjunctions to build different compound sentences.

I fell out of a tree and I broke my left arm, just below the elbow.

I fell out of a tree so I never did anything so reckless again.

I fell out of a tree but I was unhurt.

In each of those compound sentences, there is a main clause before the conjunction and another main clause after it. Each of those main clauses could stand as a sentence on its own.

Follow that pattern to build **compound sentences**:

➤ Start each sentence with a main clause from the list B–F above. (We used starter A already in the examples.)

➤ Follow up with the conjunction 'and'.

➤ Add another main clause of your own invention to create a compound sentence.

➤ Now use the same beginnings with the conjunction 'so'. Add a different new main clause to each to create another compound sentence.

➤ Then use the third conjunction 'but' and do this again, adding yet another new main clause to end each compound sentence.

HINT! You should end up with 15 compound sentences – three from each starter. You can look at the examples for starter A on page 123 to help you. Remember, you are always adding a main clause that would also work as a sentence on its own.

Well done! You have learned lots about sentences, including lots of information about sentence structure that even many very good writers would not be able to explain.

There is a revision task about sentences on page 129. You could choose to do that now, but it is probably more useful to leave it until the end of this chapter after you have learnt about paragraphs.

We don't often find sentences on their own. Sentences are usually grouped together. It's time to learn about paragraphs.

▶ Paragraphs

A paragraph is a group of sentences that share one main idea. It looks like a distinct chunk of writing on the page, because there are gaps before and after it.

There is no firm rule about how long paragraphs should be. However, is better not to let them get too long, as that can make the ideas hard to follow.

≫ Main ideas

As it says above, the sentences in a paragraph should share one main idea. If you look at the definition box, both sentences in the first paragraph are about what a paragraph is. Both sentences in the second paragraph are about paragraph length.

Building

Read these paragraphs. Identify the **main idea** of each paragraph.

1   Rain is really important. It replenishes gardens and farms. It refills rivers and ponds where fish swim and animals drink. It brings nature to life. It cleans dirt off our streets and away into the drainage system.

2   Quizzing is an enjoyable way to spend an evening. You can join up with friends and compete against each other in teams. You can make up your own rounds based on topics that you know lots about. It will bring out everyone's competitive side and be a great laugh. And, of course, if you win, you'll feel really pleased with yourself.

3   The pangolin is a fascinating creature. Although they are mammals, like dogs, rabbits or sheep, pangolins are covered in scales. In fact, the pangolin is the world's only scaly mammal. When pangolins feel afraid, they curl up in a ball, protected by their outer scales. They live in trees or burrows and eat ants, which they catch with their very long tongues. They come in very varied sizes, from as short as 30 cm to as much as a metre long.

 Strengthening

Use this mixer to help you choose a **main idea**. Then write a **paragraph** that fits that idea. Write **at least five** sentences.

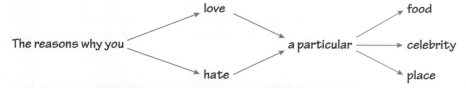

Extending

You are now going to write some more paragraphs.

The mixer gives up to six different main ideas for paragraphs. If you are using this book on your own, set yourself a goal for how many more paragraphs you will write. If you are using this book in school, ask your teacher to set that goal for you.

❯❯ Topic sentences

Many paragraphs, though not all of them, begin with a topic sentence. This is a sentence that tells the reader what the paragraph will be about: it gives the main idea, or topic, of the paragraph. You can see topic sentences at the start of each of the paragraphs in the **Building** activity on page 122.

> Rain is really important.

> Quizzing is an enjoyable way to spend an evening.

> The pangolin is a fascinating creature.

Each of those paragraphs followed on from the idea in its topic sentence.

For the next task, look at the list of topic sentences A, B and C. Then choose a level of task: **Building**, **Strengthening** or **Extending**.

A   I still remember my first day at this school.

B   I bought all sorts of things during my shopping trip.

C   The beach was covered in things that the tide had washed up.

 Building

Choose one of the topic sentences. Copy it out. Add **at least three** more sentences to complete the **paragraph**.

 Strengthening

Either write a longer **paragraph** by adding **at least five** sentences to the topic sentence, **or** use **more than one** topic sentence and write **more than one paragraph**.

 Extending

Use all of the topic sentences so that you write **three paragraphs**, and make sure that you add **at least five sentences** to each paragraph.

Topic sentences are not needed for every kind of paragraph. For example, paragraphs in stories very often do not start with a topic sentence. But topic sentences are useful when you are setting out an argument or an idea that will be supported in the rest of the paragraph with examples, evidence or explanation:

> There are many reasons why cities should be made more cycle-friendly.

> Harry Potter is capable of real bravery.

›› Why we need paragraphs

We use paragraphs – and the breaks between them – to make our writing easier to follow. If we did not split our writing into paragraphs, our readers would get lost. They would not understand our important points, experiences and ideas.

 Building

You're going to read a recipe. At the moment, it is all in one big block of text. Work out where the **paragraph breaks** should go. You could write out the whole recipe, with the paragraph breaks properly shown. (If you do that, write it on paper that you can take home, not in your jotter. The recipe is simple to make and delicious to eat.) Or you could show your answers by writing out the first few words of each paragraph.

HINT! You should end up with a heading and **seven** paragraphs.

WHITE CHOCOLATE ICE CREAM

Start with 400 g of white chocolate. Cut 50 g of this into tiny pieces with a sharp knife to make chocolate chips. Put these to one side. Break up the rest of the chocolate and put it in a bowl. Whip 450 ml of double cream in a large bowl until it stands in stiff peaks, adding about one tablespoon of caster sugar towards the end of the whipping. Separate four medium eggs. Whip up the yolks in a small bowl with a dessertspoon of warm water. In another large bowl, whisk the whites until very stiff and peaked. Melt the bowl of chocolate in a microwave or on the stove over a pan of gently simmering hot water. Once it is melted, take the chocolate off the heat and add the egg yolks and about two tablespoons of water. Beat well until you have a thick glossy yellow paste. Pour the yellow paste into the bowl of whipped cream. Spend a good long time folding this gently together until it's evenly blended. Then tip the whole lot into your large bowl of egg whites. Gently fold it together until everything is smooth. Pour the whole lot into a freezable container. Sprinkle the chocolate chips you made earlier on top and freeze the ice cream overnight. Because of the fresh cream this should be eaten within two or three days. It makes enough for about ten to twelve helpings.

 Strengthening

Now work out the **main idea** for each of your seven paragraphs.

Extending

Making a recipe is a process – a series of steps. Think of a process that you understand. It could be one from this list of suggestions or it could be one of your own:

➤ a recipe that you can make

➤ how to create a PowerPoint or Prezi

➤ how to apply make-up or create a particular hair style

➤ washing the dishes or doing the laundry

➤ checking into and boarding a flight at an airport

➤ directions for how to get from one place to another

You are going to write a series of paragraphs that someone else could follow to help them carry out this process.

First, plan your piece of writing by working out the **main idea** of each paragraph. Write these down in a list for yourself. Each main idea should just be a few words or a note: it doesn't have to be a full sentence.

Then, explain how to follow this process. Make sure you divide your writing into **paragraphs**.

>> Paragraph breaks and layout

We use paragraphs to make our writing easier to follow. However, we must use proper breaks between those paragraphs to show readers where the paragraphs actually are.

There are two ways to show a break between paragraphs:

➤ If you are **typing** your words, hit the return or enter key twice so that your device skips a whole line. You can see this kind of break between all the paragraphs in this book.

➤ If you are **writing with a pen or pencil**, you could also skip a line, as explained above. However, handwriters also have another option. You can go to the next line, but move your writing over a bit to the right, which is called indenting. You can measure the size of the gap by using your thumb or two fingers side-by-side. It would look something like this:

> They spent days simply wandering along the beach, picking up shells and exploring rockpools. Each evening they lit a bonfire and cooked the fish they'd caught that day.
>
> They were heartbroken at the end of the holiday. Nobody wanted to go home; nobody could bear the thought of life in the hot, crowded city.

Whether you are a line-skipper, or a new line and indenter, you **must** stick to that and break **all** your new paragraphs in the same way. It doesn't matter how long the paragraph is. It doesn't matter why you have started a new paragraph. If you are a line-skipper, **always** skip a line before every new paragraph. If you start a new line and then indent, **always** do that at the beginning of every new paragraph.

It is **never** enough just to start a new line. You should always be able to see some sort of gap at the left edge of your page, either an indentation or an empty, skipped line.

Mistake!

You learned how to paragraph speech and conversations on page 78. Many writers make mistakes with paragraph breaks for speech. There is no such thing as a different kind of paragraph for speech. Do what you would do for any other new paragraph by following the rule above. If you are typing, skip a line. If you are writing by hand, either skip a line or start a new line and indent.

>> The length of a paragraph

You already know that if a group of words make sense together, you have a sentence. There is no rule about how long a sentence is, as long as it makes sense. There is no rule about how long a paragraph should be either. If several sentences are all about the same main idea, they can be together in the same paragraph. If you move to a new main idea, start a new paragraph.

A paragraph can be as short as one sentence.

There are even some situations when a paragraph might be just one word:

Mia hurried along the road, keeping to the edge by the wall, away from the puddles and the passing cars. She'd be home soon. Her dinner would be ready and waiting, and then she would have a long hot bath.

'Help!'

Where had the voice come from? Mia spun round, her eyes searching the darkness, her ears tingling to hear the sound again.

It is the sense that makes a sentence; it is the main idea that makes the paragraph.

>> When to use a paragraph break

You already know that a paragraph is a group of sentences that all share the same main idea. When you have a new main idea, you need a new paragraph, properly set out after a paragraph break.

Another way of knowing when to take a paragraph break is to think about **change**. If something changes in your writing, it is time for a paragraph break and a new paragraph.

You should use a paragraph break and start a new paragraph when you change:

➤ the **place** or **time** that you are writing about

➤ what you are **describing** in your writing

➤ what is **happening** in your writing

➤ the **idea** that you are explaining or discussing in your writing

➤ the **character** that you are writing about

➤ the **speaker** in a conversation.

And you should always use a break and start a new paragraph if you begin a sentence with the word 'Suddenly', because anything that happens suddenly causes a change.

 Building

In this passage, the **paragraph breaks** that should show a change of place or time are missing. **Either** write out the passage, putting in the paragraph breaks as you go, **or** show your answers by writing out the first few words of each new paragraph.

> Monday was fine and sunny. There wasn't a cloud in the sky. I spent the whole day wandering the streets of the old city, peeping into courtyards. Whenever I got hot or tired, I stopped at a pavement café. The next day began with thick heavy clouds. I slipped a waterproof jacket in my bag and set off towards the museum. When I got there, I had to join a long queue, but it was worth it. I learned so much about the history of the city. That afternoon, the sun came out again, and I headed for the beach as temperatures soared.

 Strengthening

In the next passage, the **paragraph breaks** that should show a change of place or time are missing. So are the breaks that should show what is happening, including sudden events. **Either** write out the passage, putting in the paragraph breaks as you go, **or** show your answers by writing out the first few words of each new paragraph.

In the evening, I went out for dinner. I knew there was a square in the old town that was lined with cafés and restaurants. I'd be sure to find a good place there. As I came out of an alleyway and into the corner of the square, I heard a noise. It sounded like a crowd. I couldn't tell if they were excited or angry. They might be sports fans; it might be a riot. Suddenly, hundreds of people, all dressed in red and gold, came pouring out of the alley opposite, filling the square. I ducked down, out of sight, behind a display board covered in pictures of delicious-looking food.

 Extending

In this passage, the **paragraph breaks** that should show a change in what is happening are missing. So are the breaks that should show a change in the character being written about and the paragraph breaks that should be used in a conversation. **Either** write out the passage, putting in the paragraph breaks as you go, **or** show your answers by writing out the first few words of each new paragraph.

HINT! You can look back at page 78 for a reminder about the specific rules for paragraphing speech.

The people were terribly noisy, but they didn't seem angry. Some of them were waving colossal red and gold flags, others were blowing trumpets or banging double-ended drums with clunky wooden sticks. Then I realised I had company. A dark-haired waitress in a black linen apron was standing smiling at me. 'Ciao,' she said. 'Buonasera.' 'Do you speak English?' 'A little,' she answered. 'What's happening?' 'They are happy.' They certainly looked happy. They looked delighted. They sounded happy too. 'What made them so happy?' The waitress pointed at the flags. 'The colours on the flags are for their ... 'she paused, searching for the right word. I whipped out my phone and opened the translation app. 'Put the word here,' I suggested. She typed something, smiled and handed the phone back. On the screen was the word **neighbourhood**. 'What did their neighbourhood do?' 'Every neighbourhood has a horse. Today was the big race. Their neighbourhood won the race.' At that moment, I spotted the jockey, a slim young man in a red and gold striped shirt, being carried on the shoulders of the yelling crowd.

Bringing it all together

▶ Sentences and paragraphs

Now that you have learned about paragraphs, and the sentences that paragraphs are made up of, you are ready to revise and check your learning.

Write out each group of words, dividing it into sentences as you go by working out where to put **capital letters**. End each sentence with a suitable **full stop**, **question mark** or **exclamation mark**. Underline the **verbs**.

1   do you want to stay healthy it's not hard to do simple, tiny steps are very powerful walk for an hour five times a week sleep eight hours a night eat at least five helpings of fruit and vegetables each day you will see a massive difference in less than a month

2   the first time I heard the tune, it was the theme for a TV programme I knew of but didn't watch then I heard it drifting out of the open door of a café now the music is following me everywhere it rolls out of shops it leaks from other passengers' headphones on the bus I feel haunted I hate it

Remember, you should start a new paragraph in your writing when you change:

➤ the place or time   ➤ what is happening

➤ the idea or subject   ➤ what you are describing

➤ the character or speaker   ➤ what you are discussing.

Either write out the passage, putting in the paragraph breaks as you go, **or** show your answers by writing out the first few words of each new paragraph.

> On Friday evening, after work, I went to the dentist. I'm a little scared of having my teeth checked, but I knew it was the right thing to do. The dentist was very pleased with me. 'You've looked after your teeth really well,' she said. 'There's no need for any fillings.' Next morning, I got my hair cut. I usually enjoy that, because there are magazines to read and they always bring me a cup of tea. Unfortunately my usual stylist was off on holiday. 'Are you sure you want it to look like that?' said the stand-in, when I told him what I wanted. I was sure, but that didn't help. I came out looking as if I had lost a fight with a lawnmower. Back at home that afternoon, in front of the bathroom mirror, I took drastic steps. I shaved the whole lot off, and filmed myself doing it. Later, I posted it online with a link to the website of my favourite charity. By bedtime on Sunday, my daft impulse had raised £10,000 for a good cause. Suddenly, I'm a hero.

4 Spelling

English spelling is curious and complicated. Look at the word below. Do you recognise it? Try reading it out loud and decide what you think it should sound like.

> ghoti

This word is actually pronounced 'fish'. Here's how:

➤ The gh- comes from words like 'laugh', 'enough', 'rough' and 'tough', where those two letters makes a sound like 'f' .

➤ The -o- is from the word 'women', where that letter sounds like a short 'i'.

➤ The -ti at the end is from words such as 'nation', 'motion' and 'attention', where those letters make a 'sh' sound.

So:

> gh + o + ti = fish

Here's another famous example of strange English spelling. Look at these four words:

> cough   dough   enough   plough

They look very similar. They are all mostly made of the letters -ough. Now read the words out loud. You should hear four completely different sounds.

These slightly silly examples make a serious point. In fact 'ghoti' was deliberately invented to prove that point. English spelling is tricky because it's so varied.

Not all languages are like this. This writer lived in Poland and learned to speak Polish. Some of the words looked a little odd at first, because they had so many consonants so close together. Words like *szczeniak* (which means 'puppy') looked a bit scary. Then someone told the writer that those consonants *szcz-* always make the same sound, and they sound like the letters -shch- in 'pushchair' or 'boyish charm'.

Polish is a phonetic language, where the same letter groups and combinations always make the same sounds. English is not phonetic. There are some English spelling rules you can learn, but most of those rules have exceptions, so they are not always useful.

This chapter cannot teach you how to spell all the English words you will ever meet. What it can do is give you advice, techniques and strategies for learning tricky words and improving your spelling.

▶ The alphabet

The first step in good spelling is to be comfortable with the alphabet. If you can use the alphabet, you can use a dictionary to help you check how to spell words and how to use them.

Here's the English alphabet, in the right order:

a b c d e f g h i j k l m n o p q r s t u v w x y z

The five letters picked out in red – 'a', 'e', 'i', 'o' and 'u' – are called vowels. The other 21 letters are called consonants. We'll come back to them later.

>> Alphabetical order

In a dictionary, in the index of a book and in most filing systems, words are listed in alphabetical order. So to be able to use any of those useful collections of information you have to be comfortable with using alphabetical order.

 Building

By looking at the **first letter** to help you, put these strings of words into **alphabetical order**.

1	tangerine	orange	lemon	clementine	mandarin
2	pear	banana	apple	kumquat	cherry
3	focaccia	ciabatta	sourdough	granary	baguette
4	tiger	leopard	jackal	cheetah	panther
5	dog	cat	rabbit	gerbil	hamster

·I─I· Strengthening

Now put these words into **alphabetical order**. This time all the first letters are the same, so you will need to look at the **second letter** to work out the answers.

1	African elephant	aardvark	armadillo	alligator	anteater
2	book	baby	beard	buffalo	bird
3	cap	cup	city	clap	copper
4	dentist	daredevil	doctor	driver	diversion
5	educational	excellent	effective	eager	eccentric

 Extending

Now put these words into **alphabetical order**. This time all the first and second letters are the same, so you will need to look at the **third letter** to work out the answers.

1	abrupt	abnormal	absent	abandon	ability
2	battle	back	barnacle	banana	baby
3	clear	classical	clumsy	clipping	clover
4	ending	enormous	enforce	encyclopaedia	environment
5	fireplace	financial	fishing	figure	fibre

 Group task

If you are doing this work as part of a class or a group, here are some games you can play with alphabetical order. To make the first two tasks more challenging, try to do them without speaking to each other.

➤ Get everyone in your class or group to stand up and arrange themselves around the room in alphabetical order according to their **first name**.

➤ Get everyone in your class or group to stand up and arrange themselves around the room in alphabetical order according to their **surname**.

➤ Get the members of your class or group to say just one letter each, starting at 'Z' and going **backwards** through the alphabet.

➤ Get the members of your class or group to say just one letter each, starting at 'A' and going through the alphabet but using only every **second letter**.

➤ Pick one of these categories: things you can see in the classroom; things you can eat or drink; animals; jobs or professions. Quickly write down a list of at least ten things in that category. Swap your list with a partner and re-write each other's lists in alphabetical order. You can keep repeating this task by choosing a new category and/or a new partner to swap with.

Here's one more fun task you can do with alphabetical order.

First, write out the letters of the alphabet in order. Leave plenty of space between them, and skip a few lines under each row of letters, like this:

a	b	c	d	e	f …

Next, write out the letters of the alphabet in order again, underneath the ones you've already got, but this time move the letters forward three places. Your page will look like this:

a	b	c	d	e	f … x	y	z
d	e	f	g	h	i … a	b	c

That gives you a code key. If you wanted to write the word 'baby' you'd look at the letters in the line below and write 'edeb'.

Now, think of a message or a sentence that you would like to put into code. It might help if you write this down in normal English first.

Then, translate your message into code, following your code key carefully.

Finally, swap your coded sentence with a partner and solve each other's messages.

>> Vowels and consonants

Here's the English alphabet again, in order. The five letters picked out in red – 'a', 'e', 'i', 'o' and 'u' – are called vowels. The other 21 letters are called consonants.

a b c d e f g h i j k l m n o p q r s t u v w x y z

If you want a way to remember which English letters are the vowels, think of:

an elephant in orange underwear

Read the vowels out loud to yourself or with your class if you are at school. They are **open** sounds – no part of your mouth is shut, or touching, as you say the vowels. Read them out loud again if you need to so you can feel and understand what we mean by this.

Vowels are important because they help to build the sounds that our spoken language needs. Every word we say is made of one or more syllables – the chunks of sound in words that are like the beats in music – and every syllable needs at least one vowel to make it sayable. You can say 'apple' but you can't say 'ppl'; you can say 'education' but you can't say 'dctn'. (If you think you can say those unvowelled, unsyllabled words, you're actually just cheating and putting in some small vowel and syllable sounds as you say them.)

Two of our vowels, 'a' and 'i', are so powerful that they can stand as words all by themselves.

I like tea.

Pass me a cup.

(The letter 'y' sometimes makes a vowel sound, but it is always grouped with the consonants.)

Building

Use **vowels** to complete these words. **HINT!** For some of the words there could be
more than one right answer.

1 d _ g

2 b _ g

3 c _ g _

4 _ gg

5 b _ k _

6 m _ t _

7 f _ r _

8 fr _ _ nd

9 h _ l _ d _ y

10 t _ l _ v _ s _ _ n

11 f _ v _ _ r _ t _

Strengthening

Use **vowels** to complete this story. This time there is only one right answer for each
gap. Some smaller words have been left complete to help you.

The l_br_ry w_s qu_ _t and st_ll. All th_ books w_ r_ in their pl_c_s on the
sh_lv_s. The l_br_r_ _n t_rn_d off the c_mp_t_r and st_rt_d t_ck_ng ch_ _rs
under d_sks.

S_dd_nly there was a l_ _d b_ng. A t_ny w_m_n, _rm_d with a b_s_b_ll b_t,
c_m_ cr_sh_ng into the l_br_ry and b_tt_r_d her w_y thr_ _gh the t_mbl_ng
ch_ _ rs until she r_ _ched one v_ry p_rt_c_l_r sh_lf and b_g_n sh_v_ng b_
_ks into h_r b_g.

'N_t you _g_ _n!' s_ _d the l_br_r_ _n. 'I've t_ld y_ _ b_f_r_. J_st b_c_ _ s_
it's the cr_m_ s_ct_ _n, you d_n't h_v_ to c_mm_t _n_ to g_t a b_ _k.'

▶ Spelling strategies

We learned at the start of this chapter that English spelling is tricky because it's full of variety. Unlike languages such as Polish, English is not a phonetic language. In English, the same groups and combinations of letters can make different sounds when they are used in different words.

There are some spelling rules you can learn, but most of those rules have exceptions, which means that they are not always useful. So, instead of relying on rules to help us work out how to spell English words, we need strategies to help us learn and remember how those words are actually spelled.

›› Spelling strategy 1: read writing that has been published

Our brains are like sponges. They absorb information. The best, and most powerful, way to learn how words are spelled is to read words, to read lots of them and to read them often. If you see lots of words, you will gradually, almost secretly, learn what they should look like and how they should be spelled.

That should be easy to do, because we are surrounded by written words: in books, newspapers and magazines; in advertising billboards and posters; in texts, emails, blogs, websites and all sorts of web and phone messages. We have more written words around us than any other group of humans at any time in history.

But not all those words have been written well. The language that people produce quickly on phones or on the internet can be fast, funny and powerful. It can be clever, witty and good at building communication, but it is often not high-quality English.

So if you want to absorb correct spelling without even trying to, you need to read writing that has been published – writing that was written by someone who writes because that is their job, and then checked and edited and perfected by someone who does those things because that is their job. The spelling – and the grammar and punctuation too – in books, magazines and newspapers will always be better, and will give you better examples and models, than the spelling you find in other places.

The first step in learning to spell well is reading well.

›› Spelling strategy 2: know what you don't know but could learn

I'm sure you are already a good speller. I am sure that, when you write down words or type them, you already spell most of them correctly. Well done. English spelling is tricky, and you already get most of what you use right.

Now, focus on what you aren't yet getting right. If you are a pupil or student and a teacher or tutor is marking errors in your spelling, notice what these are:

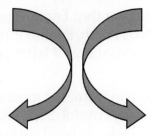

If you get the same words wrong **again and again**, make a special note of these. You could keep a list on your phone, in a notebook or at the back of your jotter. Check that list whenever you are about to use one of those words. These lists are most helpful if you:

➤ keep them quite short, with no more than ten words on the list at any time

➤ write down not just the word itself but also a short note of what it means, or a short example sentence that uses that word, so that you get used to seeing it used correctly.

If you are making **one-off mistakes** with words that you don't use often, write out the correct spelling of that word three or four times to help your brain strengthen that little bit of spelling knowledge.

You can also use the **look – say – cover – write – check** method (see strategy 3) as you do this.

The rest of this chapter suggests other strategies that you can also use to learn the spellings of tricky new words.

>> Spelling strategy 3: look – say – cover – write – check

You can use this method to learn how to spell new or difficult words.

➤ **LOOK** at the word. Are there any patterns or groups of letters in it, such as double letters or the -ough patterns we met on page 130? Does it look like a word you know already? Are there any words that you can already spell hidden inside this word?

➤ **SAY** the word out loud to yourself as you keep looking at it. Notice how certain letters or letter groups in the word create certain sounds.

➤ **COVER** the word and say it again. Try to picture the word in your mind.

➤ **WRITE** the word down from memory.

➤ **CHECK** your written version against the original to see if you spelled the word correctly. If not, go through the steps again.

Try writing down the same word again tomorrow, without looking at the original. Do you still know it? If not, go through the **look – say – cover – write – check** steps again. If you do still know the word, well done. Check the word again a week later.

>> Spelling strategy 4: use tools and supports

If you're about to write something and you want to use a certain word but aren't quite sure how to spell it, there are tools to help you.

A dictionary – in book form or online – will give you the correct spelling of a word. The dictionary also gives the word's meaning, so that you can check you're using the right word to express your ideas.

Your computer or phone will also have a spellchecker. If you have this enabled, it will underline, or perhaps even change, any words it thinks you have misspelled. Be careful! This tool is only as good as the person who uses it.

➤ Make sure your spellchecker is using **British English**, not US English. For example, in British English we write 'flavour' and 'centre' but North Americans would spell these words as 'flavor' and 'center'. Words that end with -ise in British English, like 'recognise', usually end with -ize in US English.

➤ Take care if you are using an **unusual** word. This writer wanted to use the Scots word 'oxter', which means armpit, in something she was writing. Her spellchecker changed it to 'outer'.

➤ Be careful with **names**. This writer wanted to mention a journalist called Lucy Mangan, but her spellchecker autocorrected the name to lucky mangle.

If you are using a spellchecker, you should set it to show you any possible mistakes but **not** to let it autocorrect your writing. That way you can think about possible changes and work out, using other tools and strategies if you need to, what you should change and how you should change it.

>> Spelling strategy 5: use mnemonics

A mnemonic is a memory aid where the first letters of the words in a phrase or a sentence help us to remember a wider idea. They can be used in all sorts of ways: for example, student doctors use mnemonics to learn parts of the human body.

Here are two of this writer's favourite spelling mnemonics.

Big **E**lephants **C**an't **A**lways **U**se **S**mall **E**xits

Rhythm **H**as **Y**our **T**wo **H**ips **M**oving

Remembering this mnemonic, and the picture that goes with it, will help you to spell the word because.

Remembering this mnemonic, and the picture that goes with it, will help you to spell the word rhythm.

You, your teacher or people in your class may already know other mnemonics. You can also make up your own mnemonics to help you with tricky words: just make sure that the first letter of every word in your mnemonic is a letter that spells the tricky word, and that you have them in the right order.

›› Spelling strategy 6: use memory tricks and pictures

There are lots of other memory tricks, as well as mnemonics, that you can use to learn challenging spellings. For example:

An **island** *is land* that's surrounded by water.

I will be your **friend** to the *end*.

It is **necessary** for a shirt to have one collar and two sleeves. (One use of the letter 'c'; two uses of the letter 's'.)

It can be really helpful to make up your own tricks for words that you know are hard for you. This writer used to have lots of trouble with some particular words. She couldn't remember how many letters 'e' and 'a' there were in the word 'calendar' so she came up with this:

Can you *lend* me your **calendar**? I need to see when the holidays *are*.

She also could not remember how many times to use the letter 'e' in 'independent' so she invented this:

I have a very **independent** *dent*ist.

This writer's most tricky word was 'restaurant'. She knew that she would need a funny picture to help her remember it. When she looked at the word she saw the letters -taur- inside it, and she knew that Taurus is the Zodiac sign that looks like a bull. Then she saw the word 'ant' at the end of the longer word. So now, whenever she needs to spell this word, the writer pictures a huge bull and a tiny little ant having dinner together in a really fancy restaurant.

>> Spelling strategy 7: focus on the words lots of people find challenging

Strategy 2 on pages 135-6 was **know what you don't know but could learn**. That's a great way to make an impact on words you find hard. Once you have identified the words that are a challenge for you, you can use all the other strategies we have been learning about to help you learn those words. That will immediately improve your spelling.

As your spelling confidence grows, your next step could be to practise spelling the words that **lots** of people find tricky.

In the table on the next page you will see some words that lots of people writing English often want to use and often get wrong. They have been organised into groups to make them more manageable. It doesn't matter which group any word falls into.

You could challenge yourself to learn to spell these words. Here are some ways to do that:

➤ You could start by checking which of these you can already spell and be pleased with yourself about those.

➤ You could try to learn one word a day or one group of words each week or each month.

➤ You could learn them at first by using **look – say – cover – write – check**.

➤ You could create **mnemonics**, **mental pictures** or other **memory tricks** for the words you find hardest to recall.

➤ You could make the words feel real and useful by using them in something you are writing anyway or by making up sentences specially to use those words.

➤ You could try to use two, three or four of your focus words in the same sentence, or try to get a whole group of words into a paragraph or story.

➤ You could ask someone else to test you on the words you have been learning.

Group 1	Group 2	Group 3	Group 4	Group 5
a lot	accept(able)	access(ible)	accommodation	annoyed
argument	across	achieve(ment)	address	anxious
as well	accident(ally)	appropriate	apparent(ly)	apology
beautiful	calendar	basically	column	awkward
believe	committed	beginning	discipline	daily
definite(ly)	equipment	business	embarrassment	decision
difficult(y)	excite(d)/(ment)	commission	extreme(ly)	description
disappear(ance)	height	committee	friend	different
does	humour	competitive	gradually	disease
experience	library	deliberate	guarantee	expensive
favourite	(un)necessary	develop(ment)	harass(ment)	government
immediate(ly)	neighbour	gorgeous	interest(ed)/(ing)	information
independent	possession	imaginary	mischievous	intelligent
lonely	receive	interruption	misspell	jealous
occasionally	recognise	knowledge	recommend	opinion
probably	relevant	prejudice	restaurant	opportunity
sentence	suggestion	professional	rhyme	people
separate(ly)	surprised	queue	rhythm	safety
tomorrow	weather	responsible	sergeant	sincerely
until	weird	usual(ly)	twelfth	worried

›› Spelling strategy 8: play spelling games

Playing spelling games can make you look closely at words and think carefully about them. These games make you search your memory and knowledge.

Word scrambles

Start with a long word. Use the letters in it to make as many other words as you can. If a letter appears twice in the long word, it can appear twice in one of your words. For example:

> frightening

gives you:

- ➤ finger
- ➤ fit
- ➤ fight
- ➤ ten (and so on ...)

How many words can you make from each of these words?

1	environmental	2	explanation	3	disturbance
4	unimportant	5	manipulate	6	viciousness
7	quarantine	8	abnormality	9	constructive

If you want to add an extra challenge, organise your own list of words into alphabetical order after you have worked them all out.

Group task

If you are playing this game as part of a class or group, you could:

➤ let people from your class suggest the long words that you use as starters

➤ see who can get the most new short words out of the original longer one

➤ get people to read out the words they've made, while other pupils listen and tick off those words from their own lists. Does anyone have a word that is unique to their list – a word that nobody else has thought of?

Spelling snakes

This is a game of strategy and of spelling. It's a great one to play in ten spare minutes at the start or end of a lesson.

 Group task

Divide your class into teams and decide who will play first for each team. The teacher should be at the front of the room, ready to write on a board or screen.

In this game, players spell words to earn points. Players get a point for every letter in their word, as long as they spell that word correctly.

Each player gets to choose the word they want to spell when it is their turn. That takes the pressure off individual players. A confident or brave speller could try to spell a long word to earn lots of points. Someone more cautious, or less confident, can spell a shorter, simpler word that they feel sure of.

To start the game, the teacher chooses a word and writes it at the side of the board. The only restriction is that the first letter of any player's word must be the last letter of the previous word. For example, if the teacher picks the word:

incredible

then the first player must start their word with the -e from the end of that word. If that player spells 'egg', they get three points. If they spell 'excellent', they get nine points:

incrediblegg   incrediblexcellent

If they try to spell a word but get it wrong, they get no points.

The teacher or team leader writes down how many points that player got, then moves on to the first player from the next team. In the examples above, the next new word would have to start with the -g of 'egg' or the -t of 'excellent'. Keep going, moving from team to team for each new word and always picking a new player from each team.

Some extra rules:

➤ You can't just add -s, -ed or -ing to a word that is already on the board.

➤ You can't spell a word that someone else has tried and failed to spell already.

➤ You can't spell a word that anyone can see on display in the classroom.

➤ You know that each player's word has to start with the last letter of the previous word. But a player can earn **bonus** points for using **more** of the previous word:

  ➤ Going from 'incredible' to 'egg' as in the example above gets you three points because there are three letters in 'egg'.

  ➤ Going from 'incredible' to 'blessing' would get you ten points: eight points for all the letters in 'blessing', plus two bonus points for using the letters -ble from the end of 'incredible'.

❯❯ Spelling strategy 9: learn some spelling rules and how to use them

There are some English spelling rules that you can learn. However, many of these rules have exceptions, so you cannot rely just on rules to help you. That's why we have looked at so many other spelling strategies before moving on to these rules at last.

The -qu- rule

This rule **always** works. There are never any exceptions.

The letter '**q**' is always followed by a '**u**' and then by any other vowel **except** '**u**':

quake   request   queen   enquire   quiet   unique

Write down the **'q' words** described below. HINT! The 'q' could be anywhere in the word.

1 A game made of questions
2 A female ruler
3 A slang word for a pound
4 The sound of a duck
5 A question
6 Nauseous
7 A huge meal
8 Peaceful
9 An exclusive group of people

Removing the letter 'l'

Words like 'all', 'well' and 'full' lose their second 'l' when they become prefixes at the start of other words or suffixes at the end of other words:

always   welcome   wonderful

The 'i' and 'e' rule

This is one of the best-known English spelling rules. You may have heard people say:

'i' before 'e', except after 'c', though there are exceptions.

Let's look closely at this rule and those exceptions.

The letter 'i' comes before 'e' as long as the two letters make a sound that rhymes with the word 'bee'. Here are just a few examples:

believe   piece   field   chief   achievement

However, even when the sound rhymes with 'bee', if the letters come **after** a 'c', the 'e' goes before the 'i'. Here are just a few examples:

receive   conceited   ceiling   deceive

If these two letters are **not** making a sound that rhymes with 'bee', they usually go in the order 'ei'. Here are just a few examples:

foreign   weight   neighbour   leisure   their

And, just to be even more complex, there are some common English words that don't fit any part of this rule. Here are just a few examples:

seize   weird   view   friend   species

As you can see, that famous rule is very tricky. You should decide what works best for you. You could learn the details of this rule and its exceptions. Or you could treat each of these words as a separate word that you will learn to spell correctly by using the other strategies that you already know, such as **look – say – cover – write – check**.

Words that end in -ce or -se

These words often come in two versions, as a noun and as a verb, and people often mix them up.

The -ce ending usually belongs to nouns:

advice   practice   device   licence

The -se ending usually belongs to verbs:

advise   practise   devise   license

Most people get 'advice' (the noun) and 'advise' (the verb) right, because these two words actually sound different. If you follow the patterns of those words, that will help you get the others right. Another good trick for understanding this rule is to remember that 'ice' – that lovely cold stuff you can put into a drink, or can skate on – is a noun.

Use the eight words in the box above to complete the passage. You will need to use each word once. You have been given the first letter each time to help you. HINT! You may need to put some of the verbs into the past tense.

My work at the local GP **(1) p**_____ was important but stressful. I spent all day giving **(2) a**_____ to worried patients. A colleague **(3) a**_____ me to get a hobby. I thought I'd learn to play the piano. However, pianos are large. You can't just carry one about with you in case you have a spare moment. I could hardly drive around with a piano in the back of my car. I might lose my **(4) l**_____.

I had to **(5) d**_____ a way of making time to **(6) p**_____. Then I saw something advertised online. It was a small **(7) d**_____, no bigger than a laptop keyboard but laid out like piano keys. I could carry it in my backpack and improve my skills whenever I had a few minutes free. The only problem was, I couldn't buy it in the UK. The makers were still waiting for their company to be **(8) l**_____ to trade here.

Words that end in -cal or -cle

The -cal ending usually belongs to adjectives:

magical   musical   physical   practical

The -cle ending usually belongs to nouns:

article   bicycle   circle   obstacle   vehicle

You can use this rule to help you sort out two words that many writers muddle up. The adjective 'principal' means the main or most important. The noun 'principle' means a rule or a guideline:

> When you are learning to play chess, the **principal** thing to do is to grasp the main **principles** as quickly as possible, so that you can soon start playing games.

However, there is one annoying exception. The word for the head of a North American high school, or of a British college or university, is 'principal' with the -pal ending. That's a noun using the ending that should belong to an adjective. Think of it this way. The word means that this person is the most important member of staff: 'most important' is a description, so it's an adjective, so it gets the -pal ending.

I did warn you that English spelling is tricky and that most of the rules have exceptions.

  Crossover

On page 24 you learned that some **verbs** are **irregular** when they go into the past tense. They don't follow the simple basic rule of using -ed to make a past tense.

Nouns can also be regular or irregular. Regular nouns add a letter -s at the end to make a plural. For example, 'dog' is a regular noun; its plural is 'dogs' with an -s at the end. 'House' is a regular noun and its plural is 'houses'.

Irregular nouns make their plurals in many different ways.

We need to learn about these so that we can spell them properly and also because they affect how we use **apostrophes**, as you learned on pages 70–71.

Spelling plural nouns

Most nouns add -s to make a regular plural:

    book – books   dog – dogs   plate – plates

When a noun ends with -s, -x, -sh or -ch we add -es to make the plural:

    glass – glasses   box – boxes

    dish – dishes   church – churches

Nouns that end with -f or -fe make their plurals by replacing the -f or -fe with -ves:

    leaf – leaves   knife – knives

If a noun ends in -y and there is a consonant before that letter, replace the consonant with -ies to make a plural:

    berry – berries   duty – duties   enemy – enemies

Using all the rules above to help you, turn these singular nouns into correctly spelled **plurals**. You can check back to the rules as often as you like.

1 activity	2 baby	3 blush	4 branch
5 brush	6 bully	7 bus	8 bush
9 business	10 cake	11 calf	12 clash
13 couch	14 cup	15 daisy	16 dwarf
17 elf	18 fly	19 fox	20 gas
21 half	22 hat	23 house	24 lash
25 leaf	26 lens	27 library	28 life
29 loaf	30 lorry	31 lunch	32 octopus
33 pass	34 pen	35 penny	36 phone
37 radiator	38 ring	39 self	40 shelf
41 splash	42 table	43 thief	44 torch
45 watch	46 wife	47 window	48 wolf

There are lots of nouns whose plurals are completely irregular and don't follow any rules. For example:

tooth – teeth	man – men	child – children	goose – geese
foot – feet	person – people	mouse – mice	die – dice

Some nouns don't change at all when they become plural, for example:

one sheep   two sheep   one hundred sheep   one thousand sheep

This applies to a lot of animal words, including deer, fish and salmon.

Some nouns end in an -s and look plural, or mean something that seems plural but don't have a singular, for example:

scissors	pliers	tweezers
thanks	trousers	billiards

 Crossover

Earlier in this book, you learned some other spelling rules:

➤ On page 12 you learned how to spell comparative and superlative adjectives.

➤ On page 28 you learned how the spelling is affected when adjectives are turned into adverbs.

➤ On page 73 you learned how irregular spelling of plural nouns affects the way we use ownership apostrophes.

I am sure you can see now how tricky English spelling can be. Most of the rules have exceptions, and sometimes there just aren't any rules we can use.

Remember, you know lots of strategies to help you cope with this:

➤ Read good-quality writing that has been properly published.

➤ Know what you don't know but could learn.

➤ Use look – say – cover – write – check.

➤ Use supports like dictionaries and spellcheckers.

➤ Create and use mnemonics.

➤ Create and use memory tricks and pictures.

➤ Deliberately learn words that many writers find challenging.

➤ Play spelling games.

➤ Know and use spelling rules when these can be helpful.

Glossary

A **glossary** is a kind of mini dictionary. It's a list of words with their meanings. These words are usually connected in some way. They might be all about the same subject – you could get a glossary of cookery terms or of sports vocabulary. This glossary is a list of all the important terms that we have used in this book to help us understand and use English skills better.

▶ Terms and definitions

abbreviation a short version of a word, like Dr for 'doctor'

abstract noun the name of an emotion, an idea, a value or a quality

adjective a describing word that tells us what a noun is like

adverb adds something to a verb by telling us how, when, where, how much or how often it is done

alphabet the list of all the letters used by a particular language

alphabetical order a way of organising words according to the order that their first (then second, third etc.) letters come in the alphabet

apostrophe a punctuation mark that looks like this'. It is used for contraction, to show where letters and spaces are missed out when words are combined to make a shorter word and to show ownership.

article the small words 'a', 'an' and 'the' that point us towards nouns

brackets these punctuation marks look like this ( ). They always come in pairs, and contain extra information or ideas that could be removed without changing the meaning of the rest of the sentence,

capital letter the form of a letter that is used for proper nouns, titles and the starts of sentences; sometimes called an upper case letter

clause a group of words that includes a main verb and its subject

code a way of hiding the meaning of a message by swapping some letters for others; the reader has to know how the code works to read the message

collective noun the name for a group or collection of similar people, animals or things

colon a punctuation mark that looks like this : and may introduce a list, an explanation or an example, or may create a pause

comma a punctuation mark that looks like this , . Writers use commas to separate short items in a list or to create pauses in sentences. Pairs of commas can also be used to create a parenthesis.

command a sentence that gives an instruction or tells us what to do

comma splice the mistake of trying to join sentences together by using a comma

common noun a word that tells us the name of a thing we can experience with our senses: something that we can see, hear and touch

comparative adjective an adjective that compares one thing, or one person, to another

complex sentence a sentence with a main and a subordinate clause – also called a multiple sentence

compound sentence a sentence made of two, equally important main clauses

conjunction a word that can be used to join clauses or sentences to make longer and more complex sentences

connective another word for a conjunction

consonant all the alphabet letters that are not vowels. The English consonants are every letter except the vowels 'a', 'e', 'i', 'o' and 'u'.

contraction shortening two words into one: an apostrophe takes the place of the missing letters and spaces

dash a tiny floating flat line with spaces before and after it. A single dash indicates a pause or introduces a piece of information. Pairs of dashes can be used to create a parenthesis.

definite article the word 'the', which points us to a particular noun

dictionary a book of words and their meanings, arranged in alphabetical order

ellipsis is a punctuation mark that looks like three spaced-out full stops … It can show a gap in speech or writing, or that a sentence is tailing off in an uncertain or unfinished way.

exclamation mark is a punctuation mark looks like this ! It is used to show a powerful emotion like shock or anger or to show that someone is shouting.

formal writing that is more correct and exact. It can be understood by anyone learning English anywhere in the world. Formal English does not try to seem friendly or chatty.

full stop a punctuation mark that looks like this . It is used at the end of most English sentences.

future tense anything that is written or said with a future tense verb sounds as if it has not happened yet but it (probably) will

glossary a list of words and their meanings; the words usually have some kind of connection or shared subject

grammar the collection of rules and guidelines that we follow when we speak, write, use and structure language

hyphen a tiny floating flat line that touches other letters or words at each end. It is used to join words or to show that parts of words that have been split ought to be joined together

indefinite article the word 'a' or 'an', which points us to nouns in general

indent to move writing or printing a little to the right on the page, often used as a way of showing a new paragraph

index usually found at the back of a non-fiction book, the index is a list, in alphabetical order, of the important ideas used in that book

infinitive the basic form of the verb. English infinitives are always made of two words and the first word is always 'to'.

informal is the language we use when talking to people we know well. Informal English may use slang or abbreviations. It shows more of the speaker or writer's emotions and personality.

interjection a word that expresses a short burst of emotion, such as a warning or something that is shouted out

intransitive verb a verb that just happens – it is not done to anything or anybody

inverted commas another name for speech marks or quotation marks

irregular noun a noun that does not simply add -s at the end to form a plural

irregular verb a verb that does not simply add -ed or -d to form its past tense

lower case a letter that is not a capital; sometimes called a small letter

main clause a clause that can work on its own as a sentence

main idea the idea shared by all the sentences in a paragraph. If you change to a new main idea in your writing, you need a new paragraph.

minor sentence isn't really a proper sentence. It has a full stop and a capital letter but no verb, and it only makes sense because we understand the context.

mnemonic a memory aid where the first letters of the words in a phrase or a sentence help us to remember a wider idea

multiple sentence A sentence with a main and a subordinate clause – also called a complex sentence

new paragraph shown on the page by skipping a line or, in handwriting, by starting a new line and indenting

noun a naming word that tells us the name of a thing, place or person

object the person or thing that the verb in a sentence is done to

ownership one reason for using an apostrophe: to show that something belongs to someone

Oxford comma a comma used before the word 'and' in a list to create extra clarity

paragraph a group of sentences that share one main idea

paragraph break the gap between two paragraphs, shown by skipping a line or, in handwriting, by starting a new line and indenting

parenthesis a technique that lets you drop extra information into a sentence. The information is placed between a pair of commas, dashes or brackets. If you took the information between those marks away, the sentence would still make sense

parts of speech the different sorts of words that we have in the English language and the different jobs that those words do for us

past tense anything that is written or said with a past tense verb sounds as if it has already happened

phonetic in a phonetic language, there is a reliable connection between how words are spelled and how they sound

plural the form of a noun that shows there is more than one of something

possessive pronoun a pronoun that shows belonging or connection

predicate everything in a sentence that tells us about the subject. It must include a verb

prefix a group of letters that sits at the start of a word, such as un-, pre-, ex- or dis-. Prefixes affect the meaning of the word

preposition a short word that shows how one thing relates to another in space or time, always followed by a noun or pronoun

present tense anything that is written or said with a present tense verb sounds as if it is happening now

pronoun a small word that takes the place of a name or noun and saves us repeating it

proper noun the name of a particular person or place. Proper nouns always begin with a capital letter

publish writing written by someone who writes because that is their job and which is checked and edited by someone who does those things in their job. This kind of writing uses higher-quality, more accurate English.

punctuation the little tiny marks, lines and dots that we use to organise and structure our writing

question a sentence that asks something

question mark a punctuation mark that looks like this ? . It is used at the end of a sentence that asks a question

quotation words borrowed from another writer or speaker

quotation marks another name for speech marks or inverted commas, these punctuation marks are usually used to surround words that have been quoted from another writer

quote to borrow and use words from another writer or speaker

reflexive pronoun a pronoun ending in -self or -selves, used when a sentence has the same subject and object

regular verb a verb that follows a pattern and that forms its past tense by adding -ed or -d

semi-colon a punctuation mark that looks like a dot above a comma. It is used to join two sentences that have closely connected ideas or to separate phrases in a complex list

sentence a sequence of words that make sense together, starting with a capital letter and ending with a full stop, question mark or exclamation mark

singular the form of a noun that shows that there is just one of something

slash a thin line that looks as if it is falling over towards the right of the page. This punctuation mark is used to suggest alternatives or choices and often in the expression 'and/or'.

speech marks these are also called quotation marks or inverted commas and look like this ' ' . They go round the exact words said when someone speaks or they go round the words quoted when a quotation is used.

spellchecker a computer program that checks for spelling mistakes and highlights or corrects them

spelling knowing how to spell a word means you can put the right letters in the right order, so that everyone who reads it can understand which word you are using

statement a sentence that gives information or an opinion

subject the person or thing that does the verb in a sentence

subordinate clause a clause that cannot work as a sentence on its own

suffix a group of letters that sits at the end of a word, such as -ible, -tion, -ly or -able. Suffixes affect the meaning of the word.

superlative adjective an adjective that tells us that something is the most or best that it can be

syllable the individual chunks of sound in a word, a bit like beats in music

tense adds the idea of time to a verb. Tenses let us know if something happened in the past, is happening now in the present or will happen in the future.

topic sentence a sentence that is usually found at the start of a paragraph and makes clear what the paragraph will be about

transitive verb a verb that is done to something or somebody

upper case another name for capital letters

verb a doing word that tells us about action, about being and having, or about feelings. Verbs are very important because we need a verb to make a proper sentence

vowel the letters 'a', 'e', 'i', 'o' and 'u' in the English alphabet. Each English syllable contains a vowel sound.